THE ART OF BEING ALIVE

A Photo Essay on Living a Vibrant Life

The Photography and Reflections of Suzette McIntyre

Copyright 2021 by Suzette McIntyre
All rights reserved

The Art of Being Alive
Printed in the United States of America
IngramSpark/Lightning Source
First printing, 2021
All photos and passages in this book are copyrighted and owned by the author, Suzette McIntyre.
This book or any portion thereof may not be reproduced or used in any manner without her written permission.
www.photographybysuzette.com

ISBN - 978-0-578-78833-3

Other works
Available on Amazon

 BEAUTY SURROUNDS US -2016

 THE PATHS WE TAKE -2017

 REFLECTION -2018

Table of Contents

Foreward..2

Chapter 1: Seasons...5

Chapter 2: Nature..31

Chapter 3: City Streets...57

Chapter 4: Misfit..81

Chapter 5: Water...109

Chapter 6: High Plains.......................................135

Chapter 7: People..161

Author Page..186

Acknowledgments..187

FOREWARD

I almost didn't write this book because of fear.
...fear that it was wrong somehow.
Fear that I shouldn't veer from what I've always been told to believe.
Fear that I would offend.
Fear that it would look as though my depths weren't connected to my heights,
and that it wasn't right to look curiously upon other belief systems.

But then I let it go and let it flow.
Realizing it will land where it may.

You see, this is a great big world, and we're all different.
We believe in different realities, and we're on different paths, yet we're unified.
We're joined at a point within ourselves.
We're joined at the point of belief in an Ultimate Goal:
Oneness with an Infinite Power, The Universe, God, ...the Absolute.

I've spent decades exploring, journaling, reading, and freewriting to gain answers about this eternally elusive topic. THE ART OF BEING ALIVE is a result of those years of searching. Through words and images, and based on the insights gained during the exploration, I hope to help you discover the significance of this Universal Power within you and the impact it can have on your life.

It isn't easy living through the challenges life offers, trying to balance the pains and pleasures. Most of the time, we're in survival mode, existing, just getting through the day. Making it through these daily highs and lows is a necessity, but being ALIVE through it all is an art, and it comes from trusting there's a Greater Power guiding you from within.

My years of exploring revealed to me that living a vibrant life isn't based on what I do but for WHO I do it. This life isn't about me, but in order to go out and face each day, I've learned that I need to feed myself first. I need to sink deep and listen to the Universe within me, and then let what I hear *'dwell in me richly '* as I move through the day.

By honing, chiseling, and breaking through the barriers, I hope this book will take you deep to the stillness of your Source and then back out into the world with Confidence, Vibrancy, and Knowing.

Enjoy!

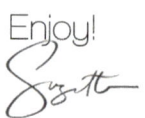

a·live{ə-ˈlīv} *adj.*
1. having life; living; existing; not dead or lifeless.
2. having the quality of life; vivid; vibrant.
3. full of energy and spirit; lively, alert.

SEASONS

An essential element to living fully alive is opening up by letting go.

Releasing is easier said than done, but we can take some lessons from the consistent repetition of nature: dawn follows darkness, flow follows ebb, winter turns to spring, birds return, flowers bloom.

This steady assurance helps us to trust nature and let go season by season, knowing each will return.

This consistent rhythm of nature day by day, year by year, is a reminder for us also to release; Let go of what no longer serves us as gently as a tree surrenders its leaves, preparing for a new season.

Embrace change.

The art of being alive is letting go of the old to receive the new.

"If you wish to fly you must let go of the things that weigh you down."
~Toni Morrison

Sometimes it's hard to let go of resentment,
but the only person this gripping hurts is you.
Clear your mind. Clear your soul.
Lighten your load, so you're free to roam.
Watch, listen, learn.

If you're clear, your Inner Guide will lead you.
If you're blocked, you'll stagnate in misery.

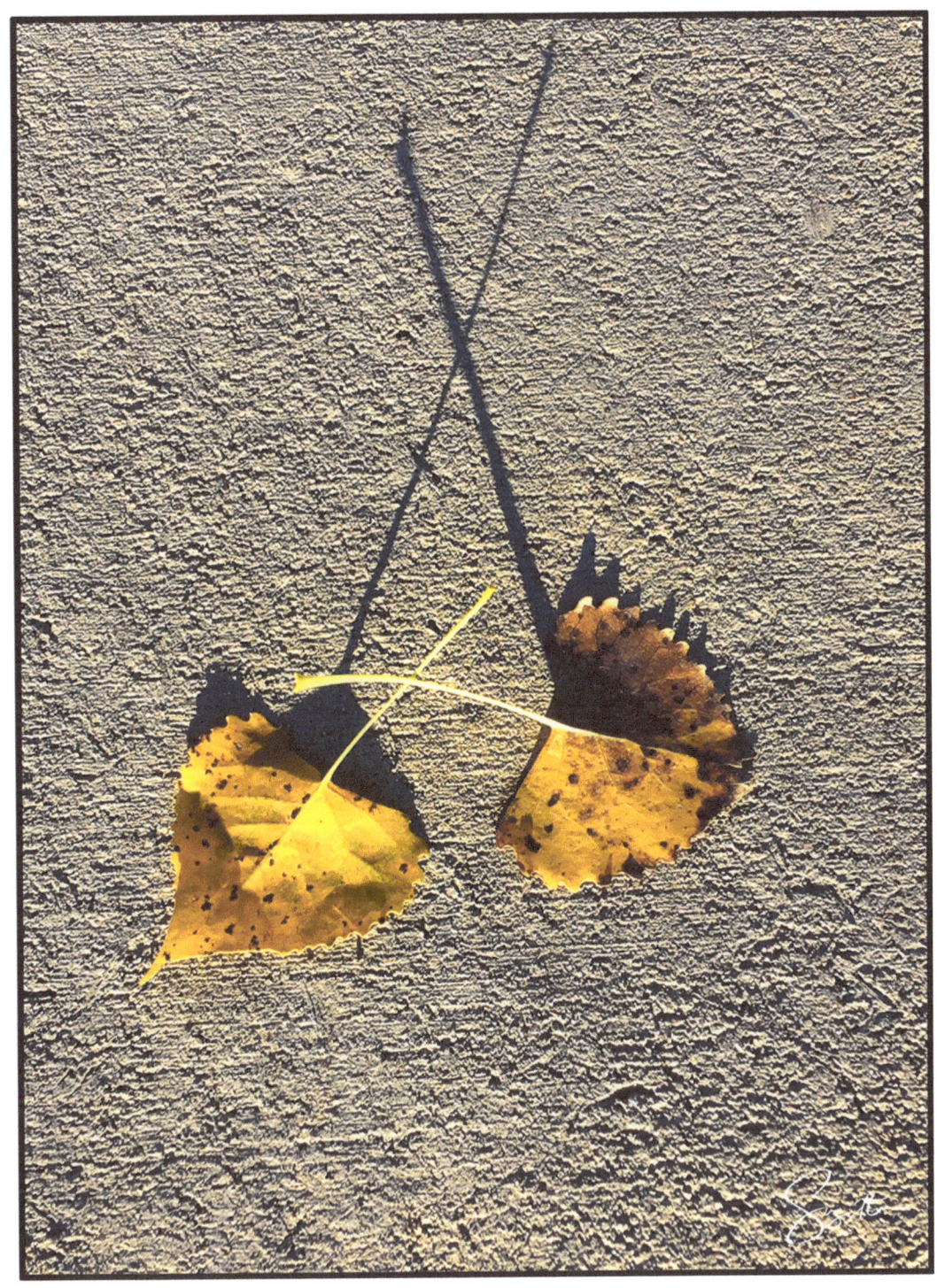

"You can't move forward if you're still hanging on."
~Sue Fitzmaurice

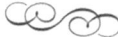

I live in a magical place - a valley near the foothills of the Rockies, and it's often mystically cloaked in fog.

Fog is one of my favorite times to work, as Mother Nature creates her own abstracts.

After shooting a few images here that morning, I drove a half-mile up the road and burst into magnificent rays of sun with Longs Peak towering into a crystal blue sky.

Our lives are like this. There are times when you can only see a few feet in front of you. Keep moving forward anyway. Clarity lies ahead.

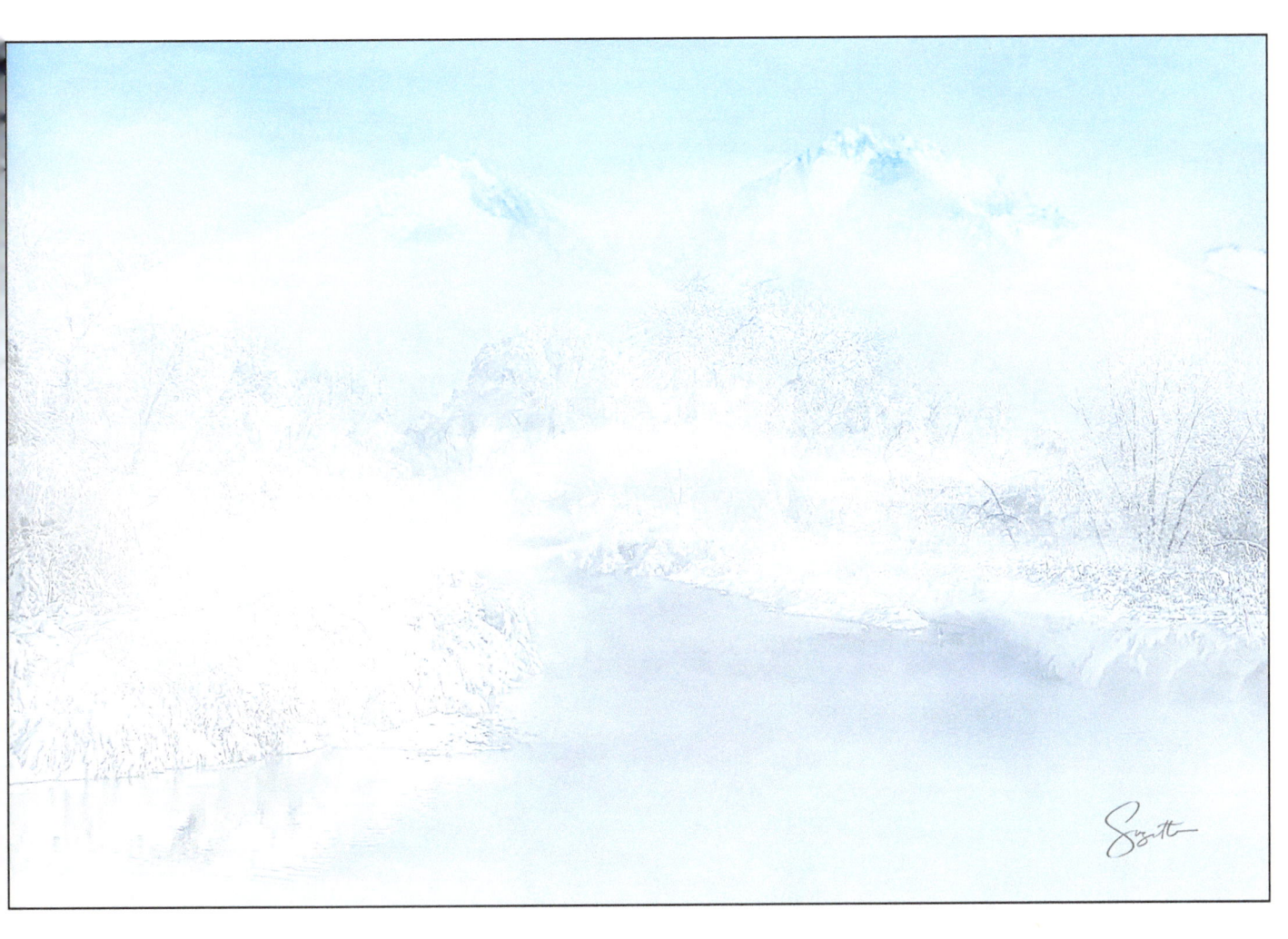

"Life moves on and so should we."
~Spencer Johnson

Many thoughts occupy your mind at any given time.
Most of them are useless and destructive.

Empty those thoughts from your mind
feel how it expands your inner space.

Feel how it calms you
and gives you a peaceful internal existence.

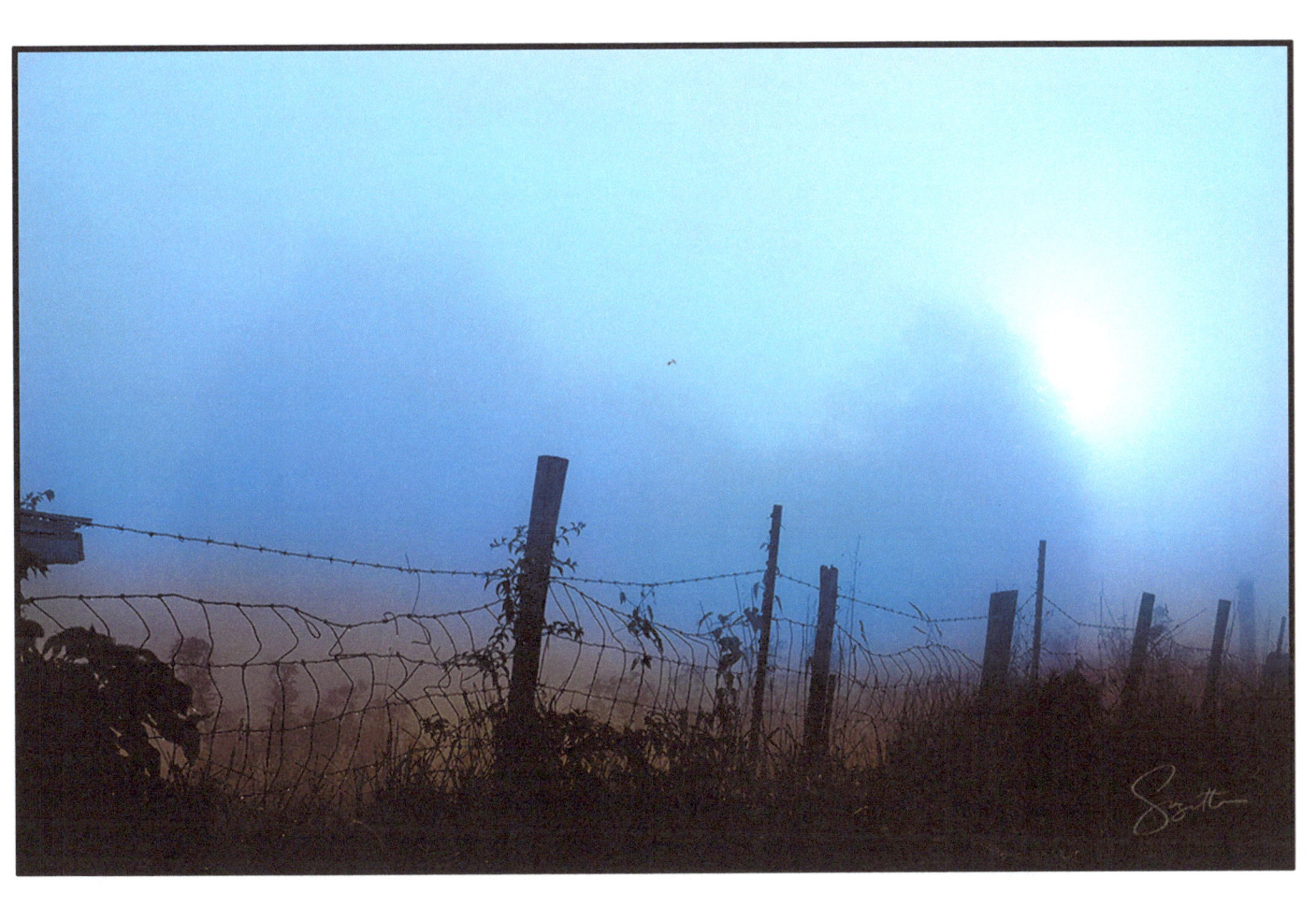

"Let go of the battle. Breathe quietly and let it be."
~Jack Kornfield

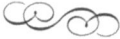

I ventured out in a snowstorm with my camera.
It was cold and quiet.

As I began to shoot, I felt heaven in the misty sunrise
and heard it through the birds camouflaged in the trees.

Just as the heavy fog masked my sight this morning,
heaven also cannot be seen.

It presents itself in every moment, though,
sometimes speaking as quietly as the song of an unseen bird
or the gentle rustle of the branches in the trees.

Trust that you are protected.
Move forward and embrace all the blessings that lie ahead.

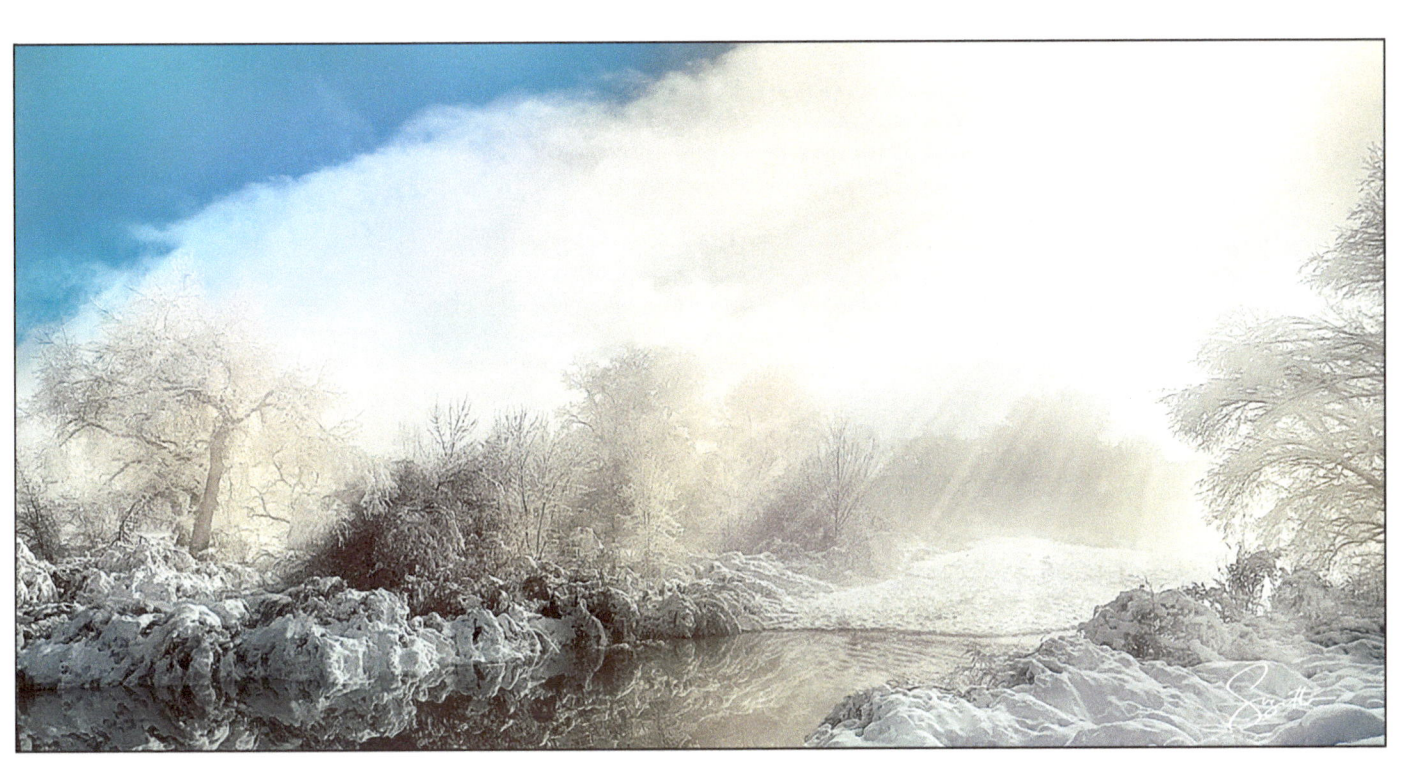

"Heaven is under our feet as well as over our head."
~Thoreau

This is a photo of my mom's old chicken coop. Many intriguing memories were created there, but we needed to tear it down along with the rest of the property's buildings.

The decision to raze the buildings was excruciating and I had to release the emotional hold I had on it to follow through. After years of vacancy and neglect, the choice became necessary to prepare the land for future growth.

Life is like this.

There are parts of us that are lifeless and neglected, yet we hold tight, not wanting to let go of what no longer serves us. The familiar weaves a comfort zone, and we become stagnant.

It would be so much easier to let go if we could understand that the release creates a threshold for all things new.

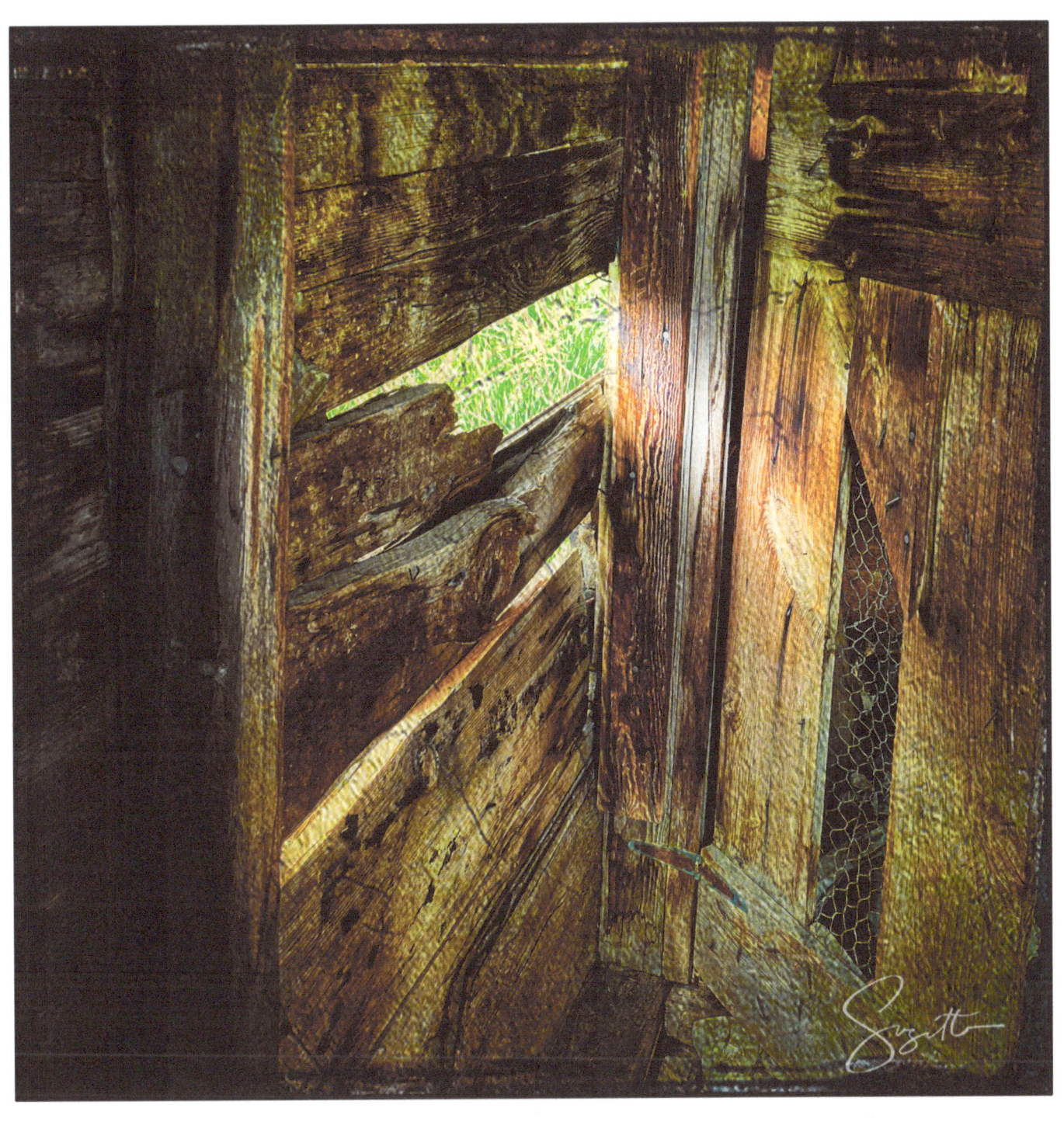

"It doesn't take a lot of strength to hang on. It takes a lot of strength to let go."
~J.C. Watts

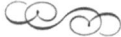

I love to shoot right after a gentle rain.

On this particular morning, the fields sparkled with fresh dew. Looking at the grasses through my camera, I noticed with a slight shift of my lens, a speck of sunlight appeared through the dewdrops, transforming the scene from mediocre to extraordinary.

That morning I had an epiphany about my own life. Any situation on earth can be mediocre or meaningless, but a slight shift of attention on my part can transform the circumstance into a surprising outcome.

Attention to the moment creates the presence of wonder.

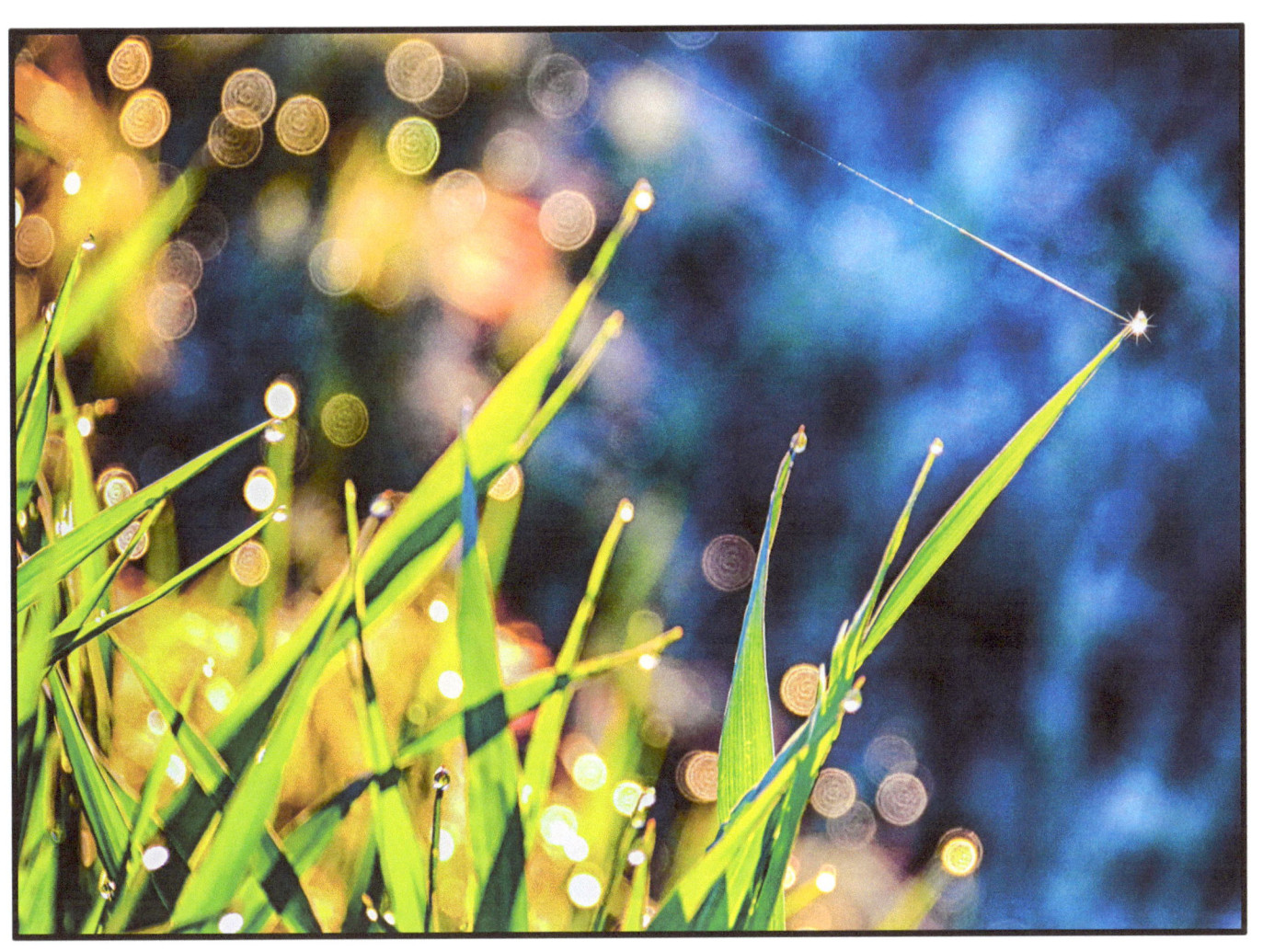

"Let your life dance lightly on the edges of time like dew on the tip of a leaf."
~Rabindranath Tagore

Allow life to flow in and through you
with no boundaries to separate you from anything else.

Tension develops when you separate yourself from your Source.

Slip into the realm of no physical separation,
a place where there is no pressure, no anxiety, just an unexplainable peace.

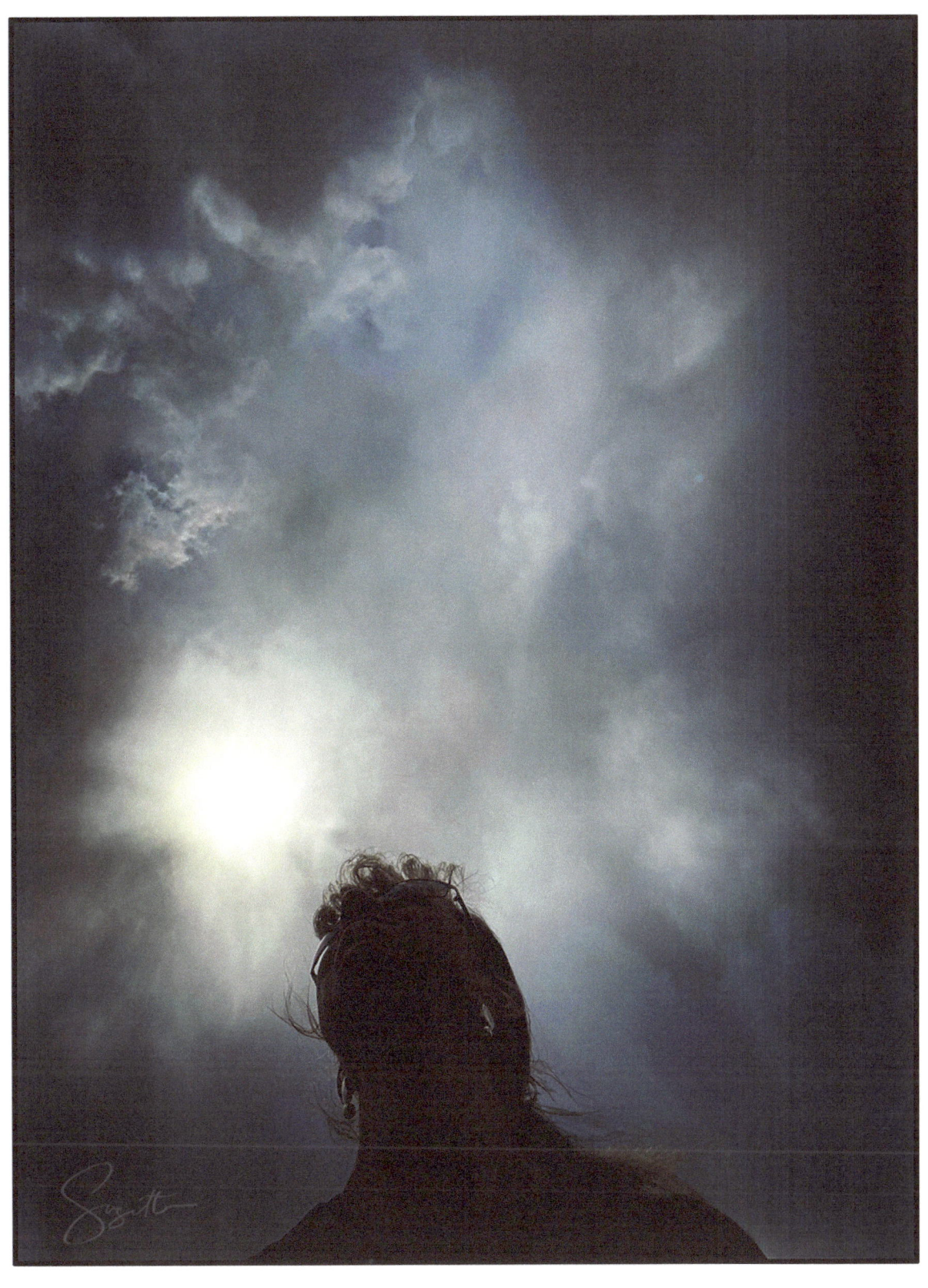

"You don't look out there for God, something in the sky, you look in you."
~ Alan Watts

Sometimes I spend much of my precious time
giving into satan's negative influence.
He torments and wins my attention.
When my mind consumes me with regret and fear,
he knows I shut my Source out.

Move inward to that deep place
where it's just you and your Soul;
your Inner Power, your absolute Heart.

You choose your thoughts moment by moment,
every day of your life.
Listen to your Source and be at peace
or submit to the torment within.

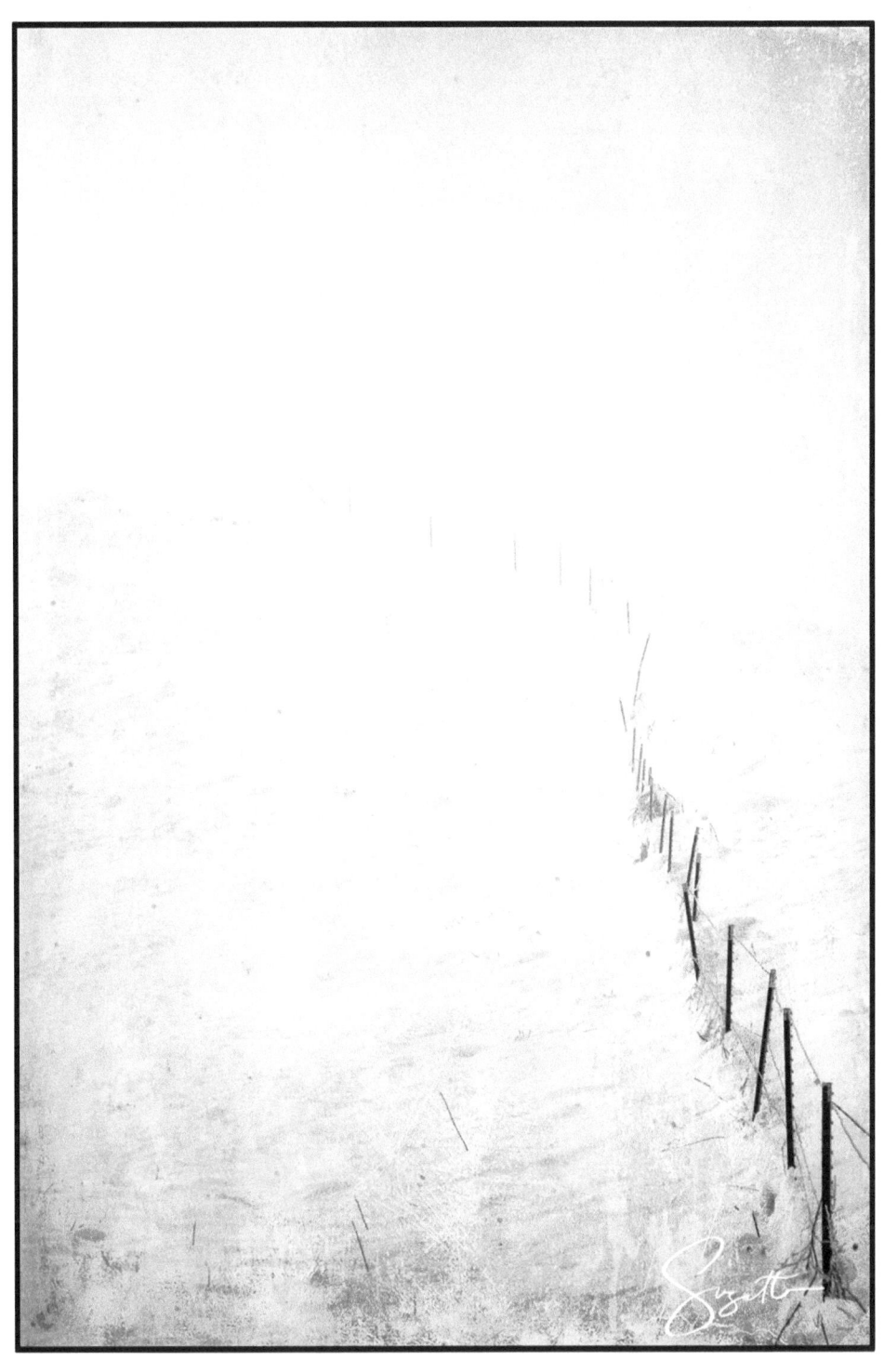

"Death is not the greatest loss in life.
The greatest loss is what dies inside us while we live."
~Norman Cousins

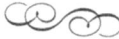

I like my alone time. In fact, most of the time I'd rather stay here in the ease of silence and contemplation than venture out into the day.

We can't sit in seclusion forever though. The world out there needs you. Insights gained from solitude cultivate the wisdom to hold you up, give you strength and guide you to where you need to be.

Step out and begin the day.

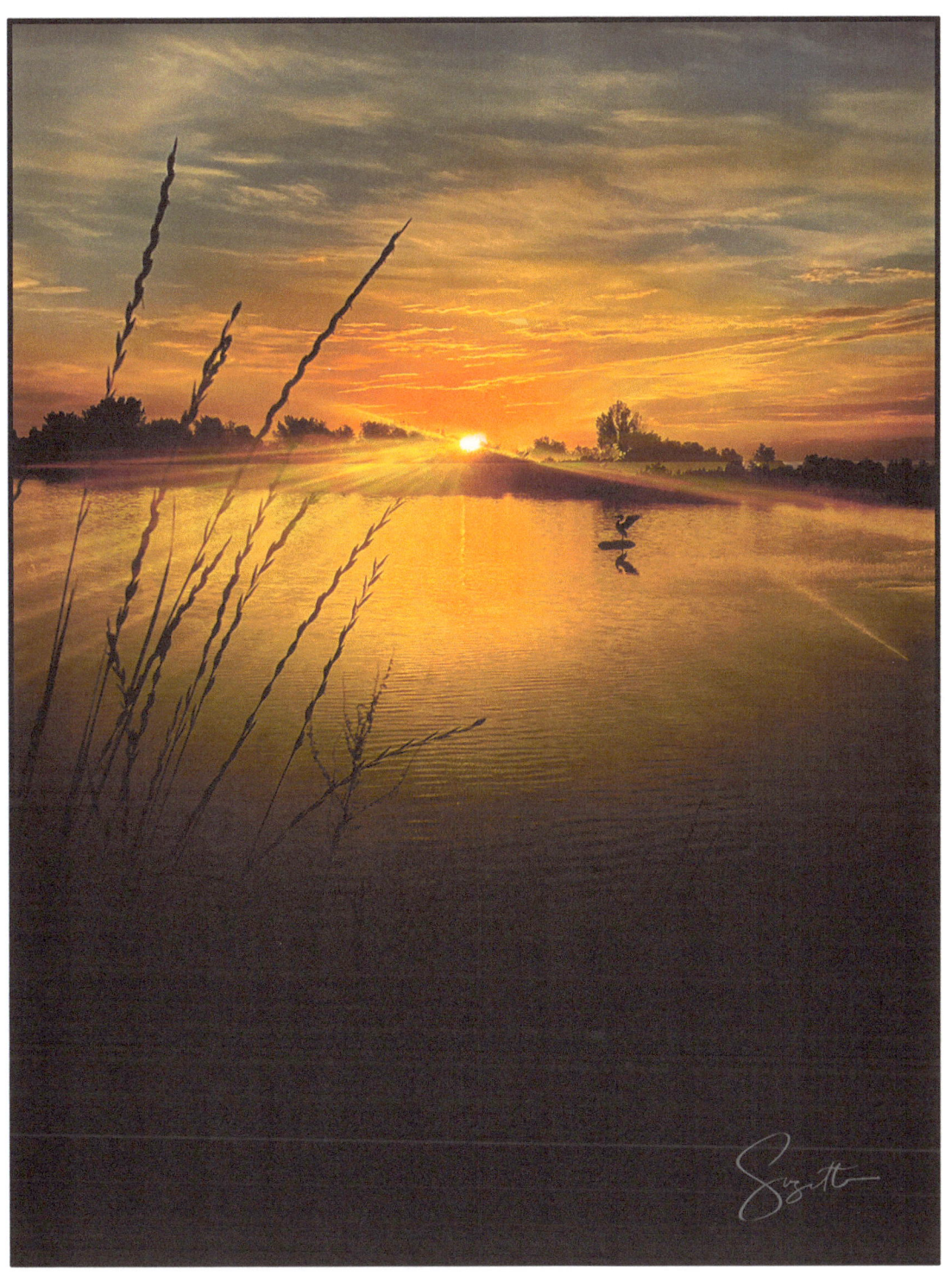

"Every moment of your life, including this one, is a fresh start."
~B.J. Marshall

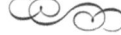

Holding on to things and lingering in regret is a burden.
Release. Let go.
Untangle from the darkness
and create a pure conduit to your Source.

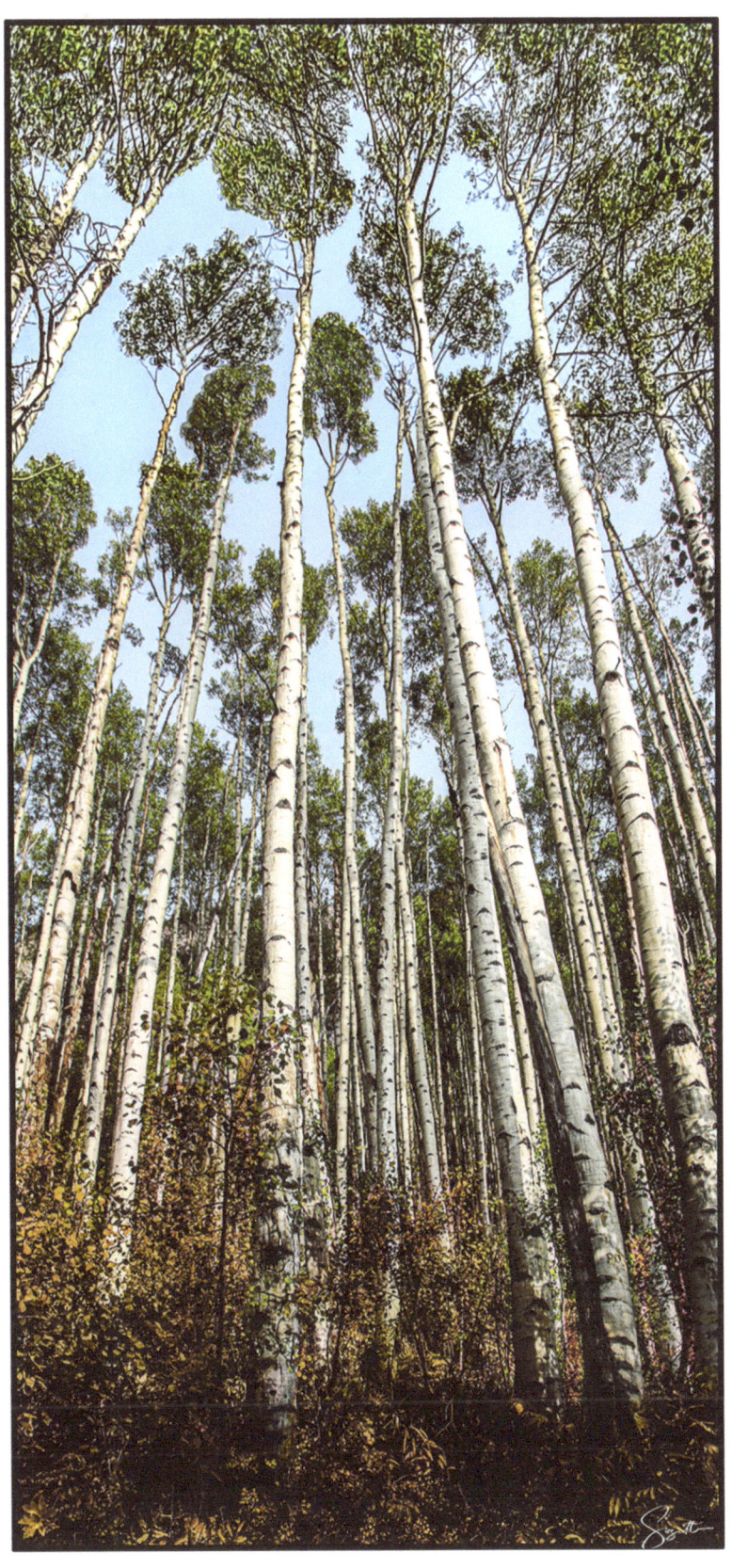

*"Life moves forward.
The old leaves wither, die, and fall away,
and the new growth extends forward into the light."*
~Bryant McGill

Shooting in the fog is advantageous.
It diminishes all color and incidental influence,
and only the most dominant visual remains.

When I'm out shooting in conditions like this
and take the time to look deep into the mist,
it rewards me with pleasing results.

Life is like that.

We go through our days in survival mode,
blind to anything but trying to stay alive.
In doing this, we lose sight of what's right there in front of us,
calling to us, showing us the answers that have been there all along.

Whenever you can,
take the time to let go of some things that are holding you back,
look deep into where you are and allow the unveiling to begin.
Let go and see.

"When there's nothing to see, look again."
~Suzette

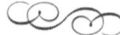

We have a limited time here,
yet we all roam around as if we will live forever.
Life on earth is not eternal,
and time slips away quickly if we aren't focused on why we're here.

Get on with it.

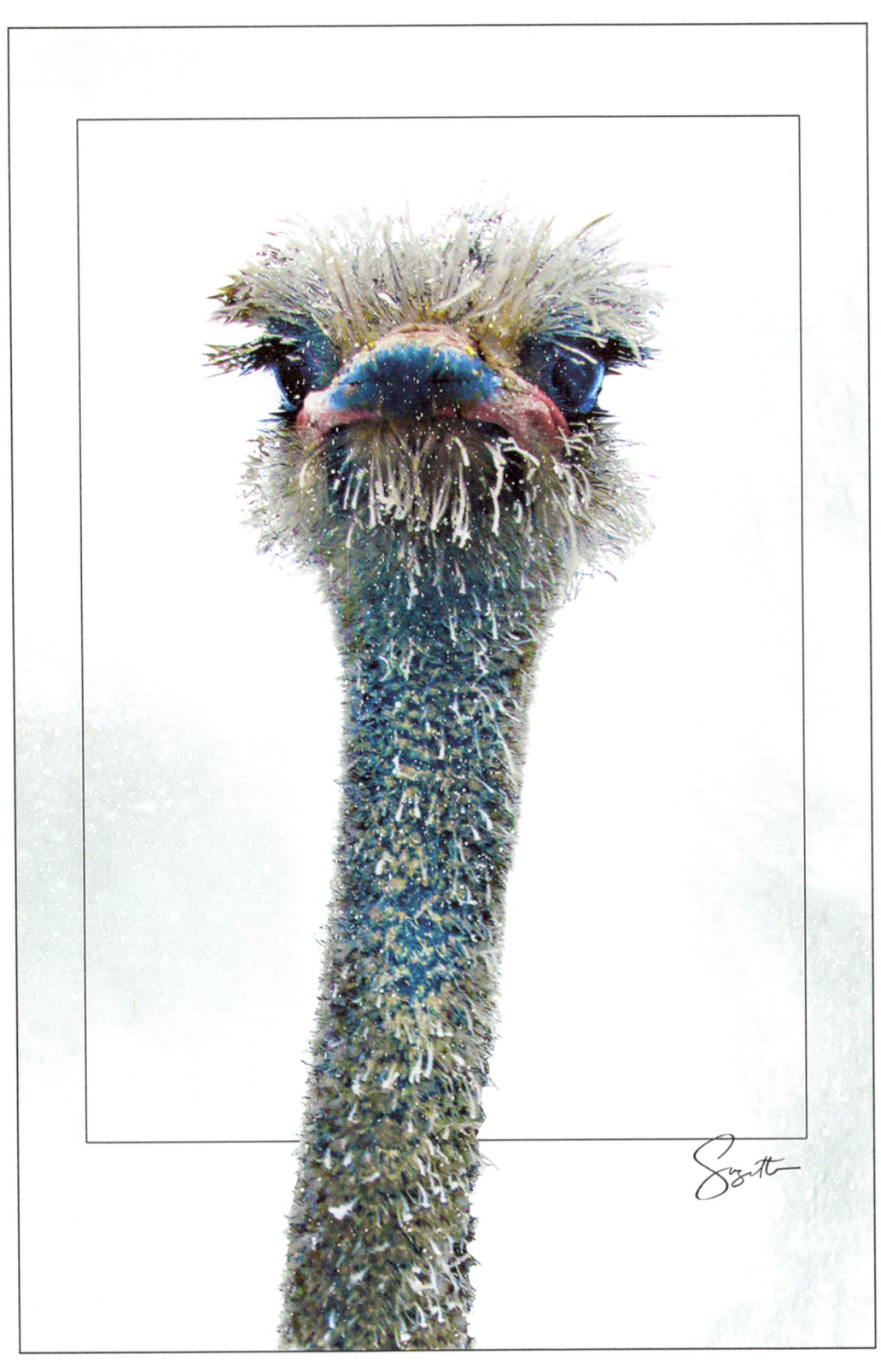

"Get on with living and loving. You don't have forever."
~Leo Buscaglia

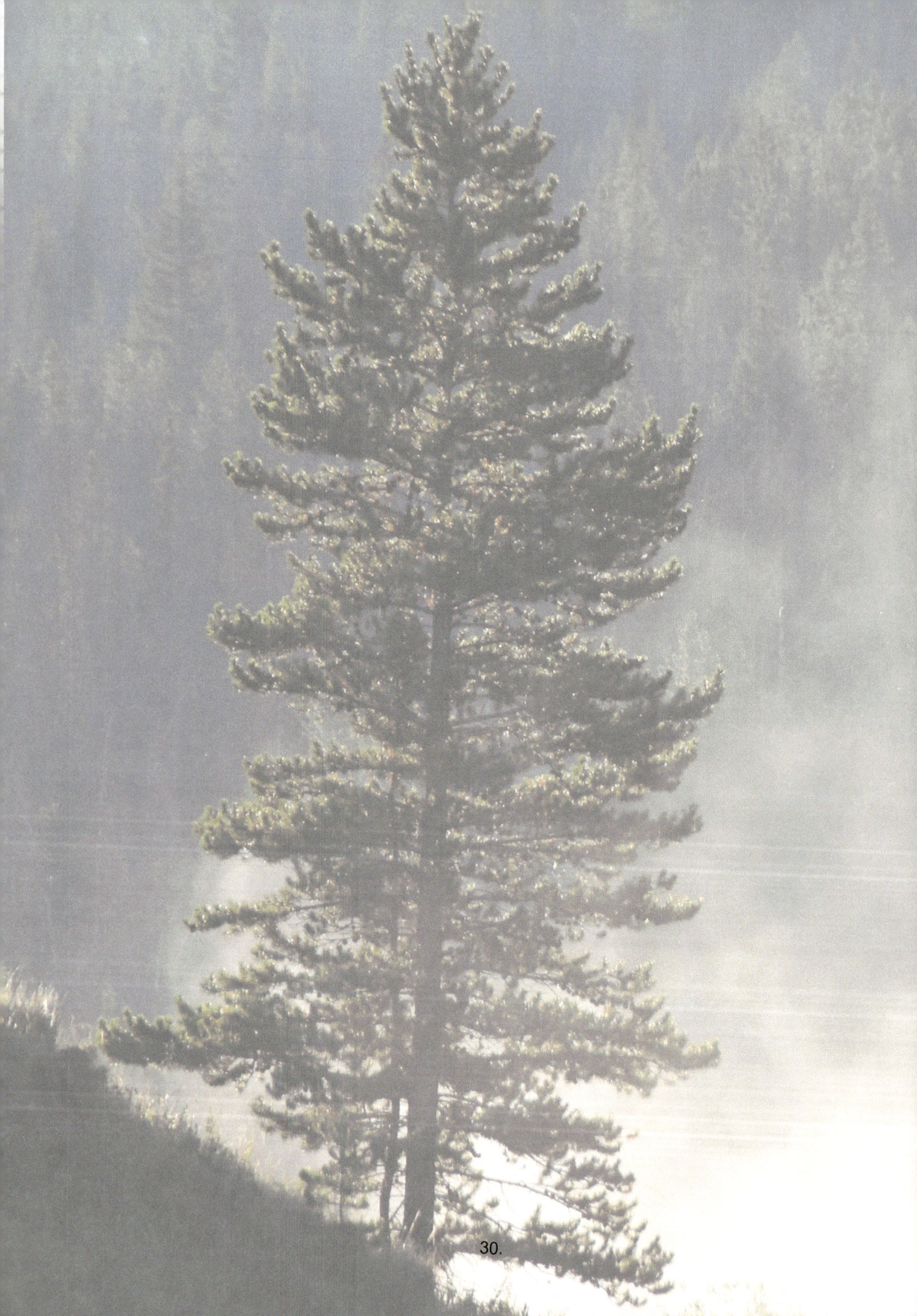

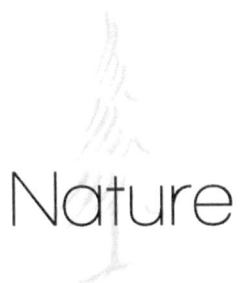

Nature

Once you've let go of some things that have been holding you back, a walk in nature can be the fastest way inward.

The fresh mountain air, the trees, and the rich earth below have a way of breaking through the mind and launching themselves deep within.

The art of being alive is matching your nature with the peace of nature.

"And into the forest I go to lose my mind and find my soul."
~John Muir

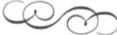

When I slip away into the mountains, I realize
how far away from myself I've gone.

There's an energy that lies in nature.
A calming Spirit that lies within the birds, the rocks, and the trees.
A Spirit that helps me connect to my Source
so that I can reconnect to myself.

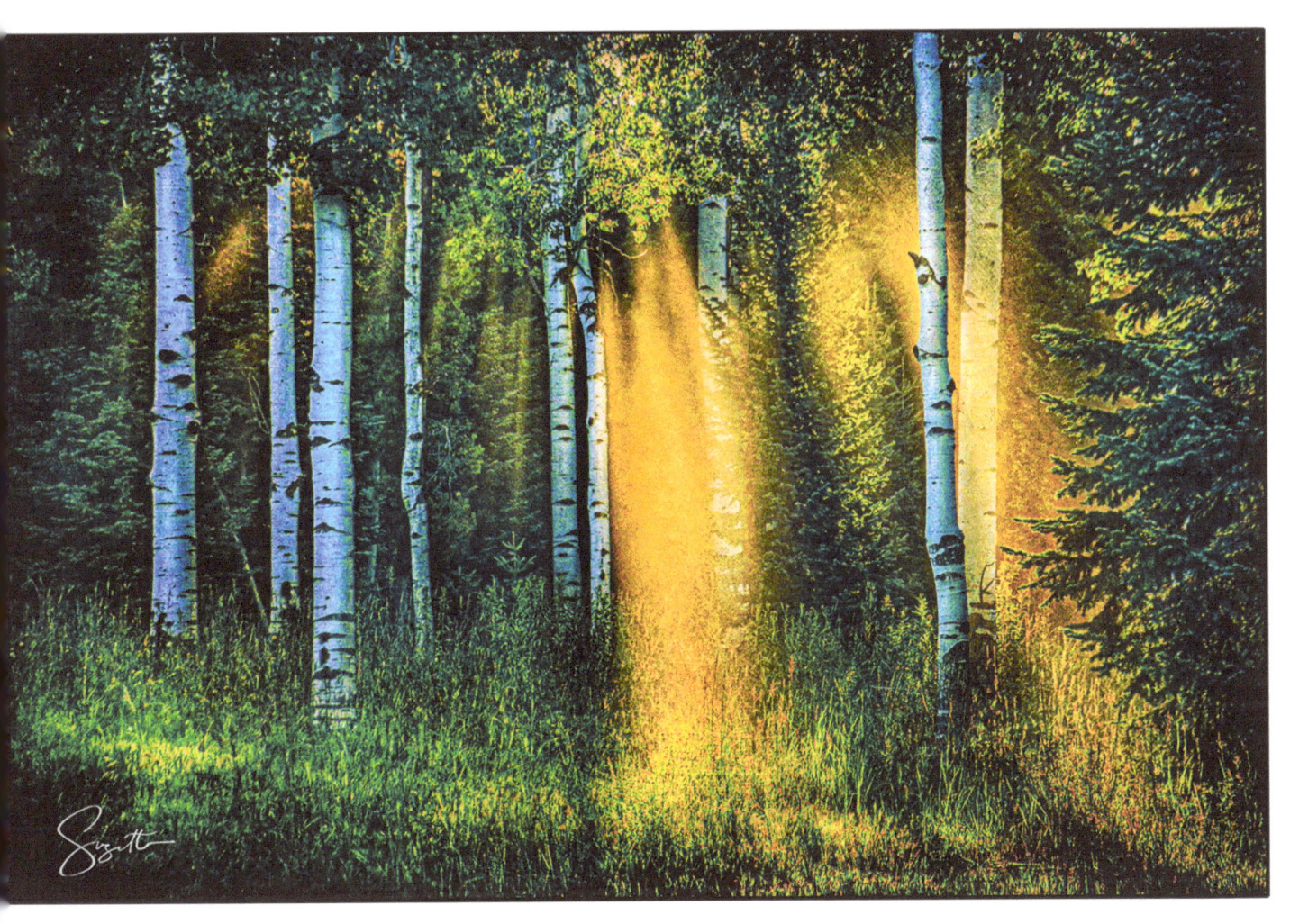

"Nature is not matter only, she is also spirit."
~Carl Jung

We become too
complicated,
spending too much time
trying to hurry things.

By doing this,
we miss what lies before us.

Allow everything
to come in its own time.
Don't charge ahead
and compromise the music
of the present moment.

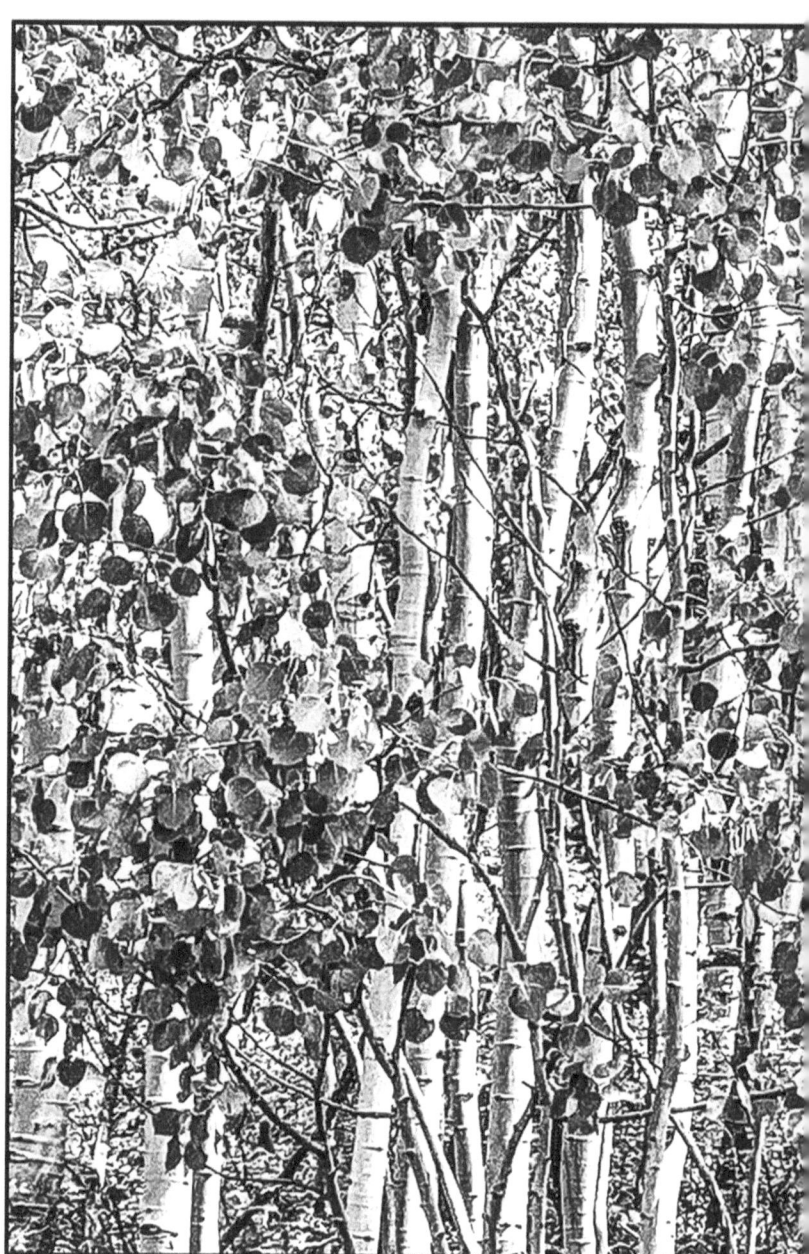

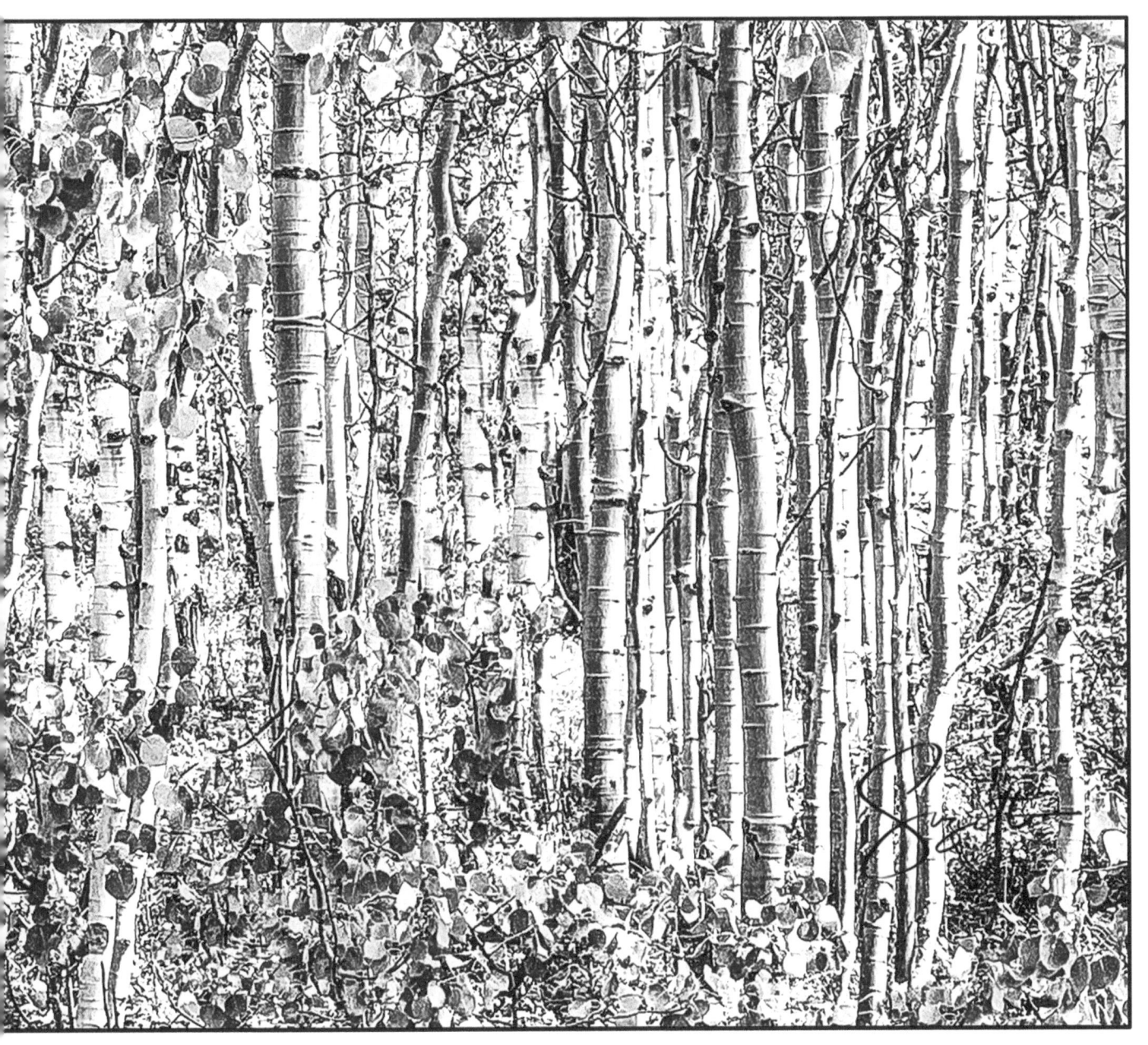

"There is always music amongst the trees, but our hearts must be very quiet to hear it."
~Minnie Aumonier

Stillness is not idle.
Stillness is full.
Stillness creates fertile ground to hear.
In the tranquility of these precious moments, sink deep and listen.
Answers harbor themselves within the infinite depths of your awareness.

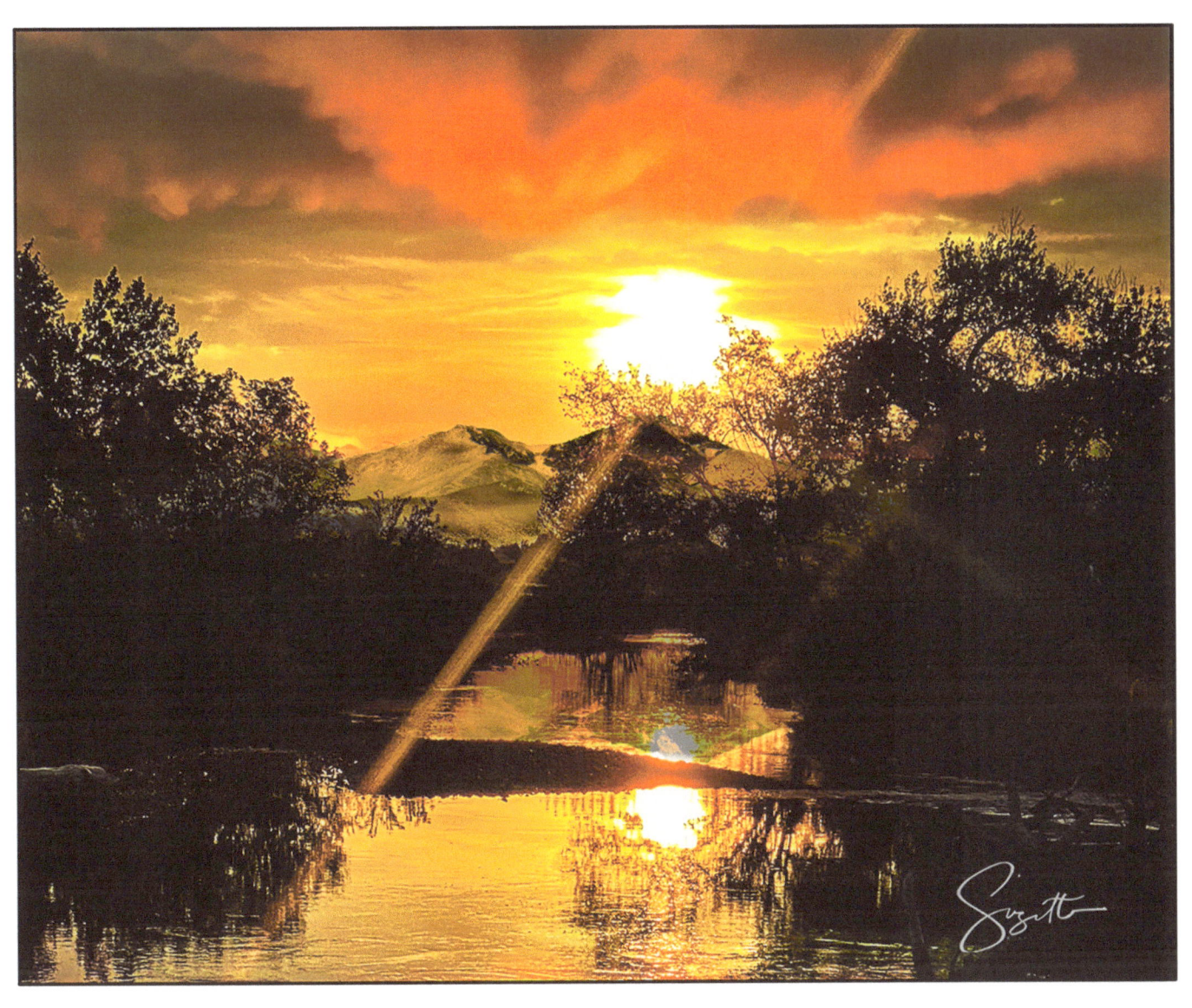

"The breezes at dawn have secrets to tell you. Don't go back to sleep."
~ *Rumi*

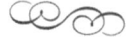

Thoreau said it well. He spent years alone in the woods of Walden Pond and became a prolific philosopher and writer.

With no distractions from the outside world to intervene, thoughts can fly free and flow into pure clarity.

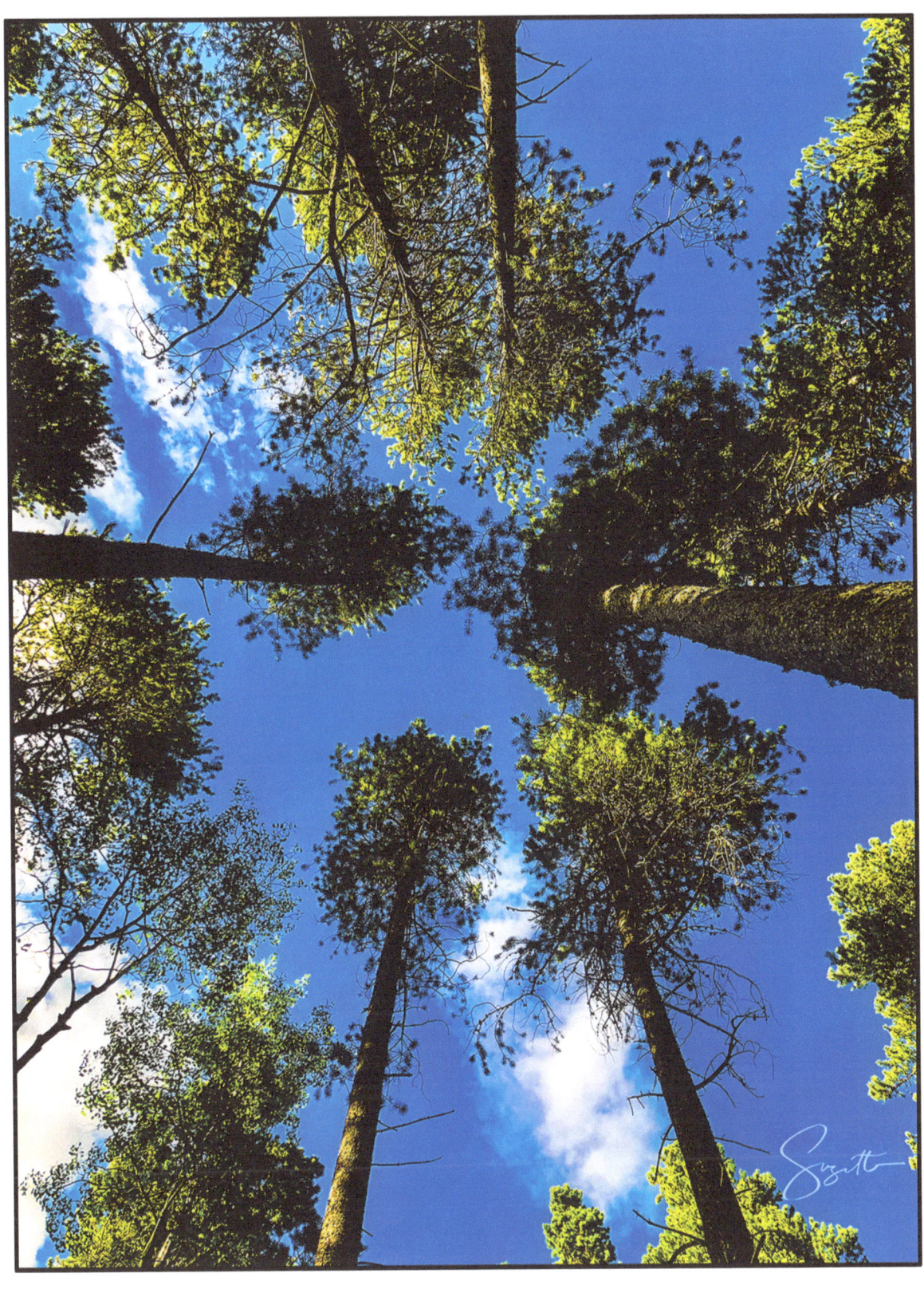

"I took a walk in the woods and came out taller than the trees."
~Henry David Thoreau

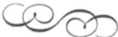

Nature has a way with herself.
She towers high and bends low.
She sails with the wind and flows with the streams.
She's complex in all her simplicity and gentle in all her strength.
Nature is never lacking.
She needs nothing more than the immediate moment
and we feel powerful in her presence as she remains solid to her roots.

By discovering nature, I discover who I want to be.

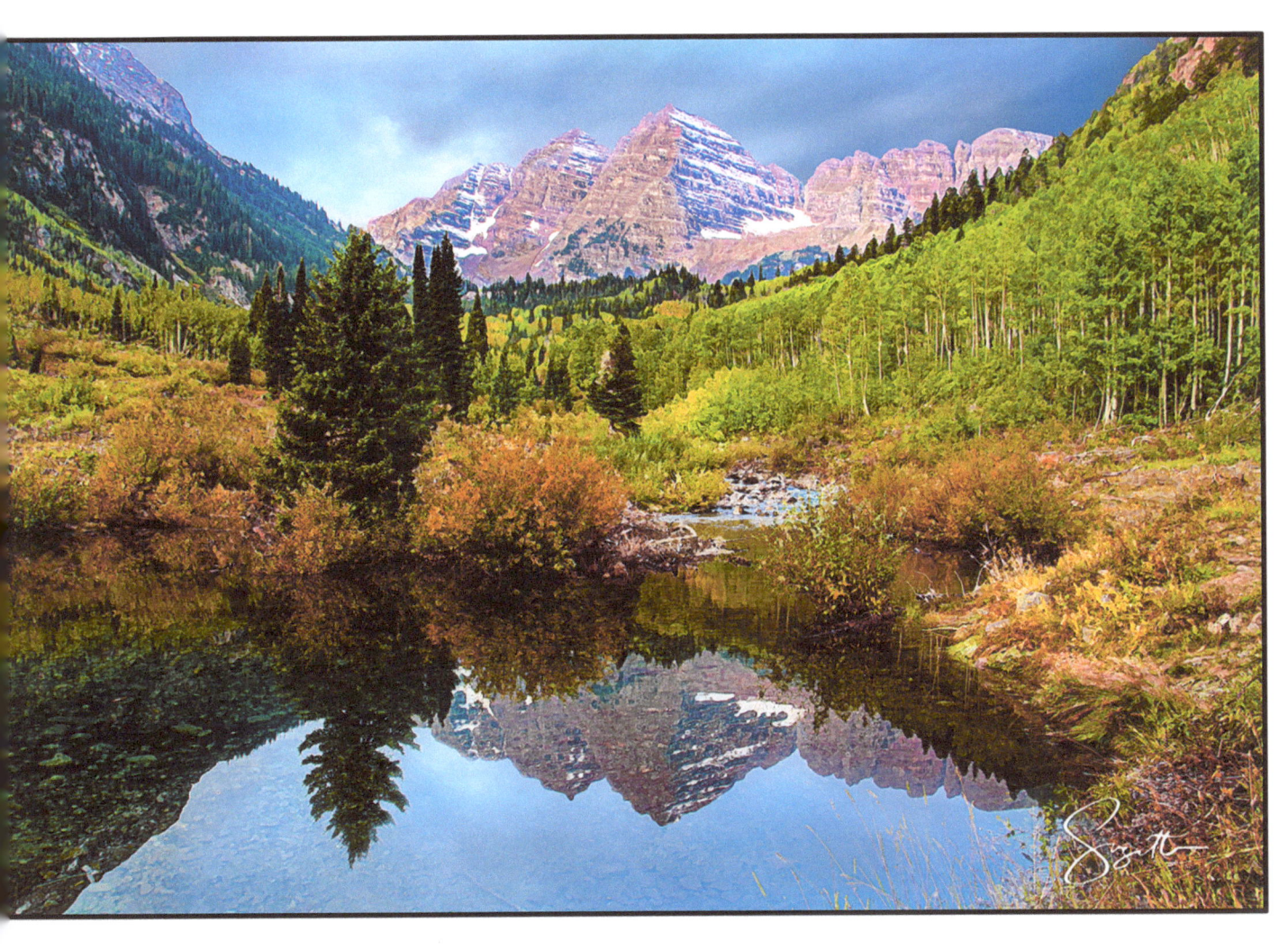

"By discovering nature, you discover yourself."
~Maxime Lagacé

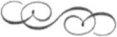

When I'm too consumed and need clarity, I escape to a quiet mountain top.
There's something about nature and all her flowing intricacies
that help me untangle thought
and realign myself.

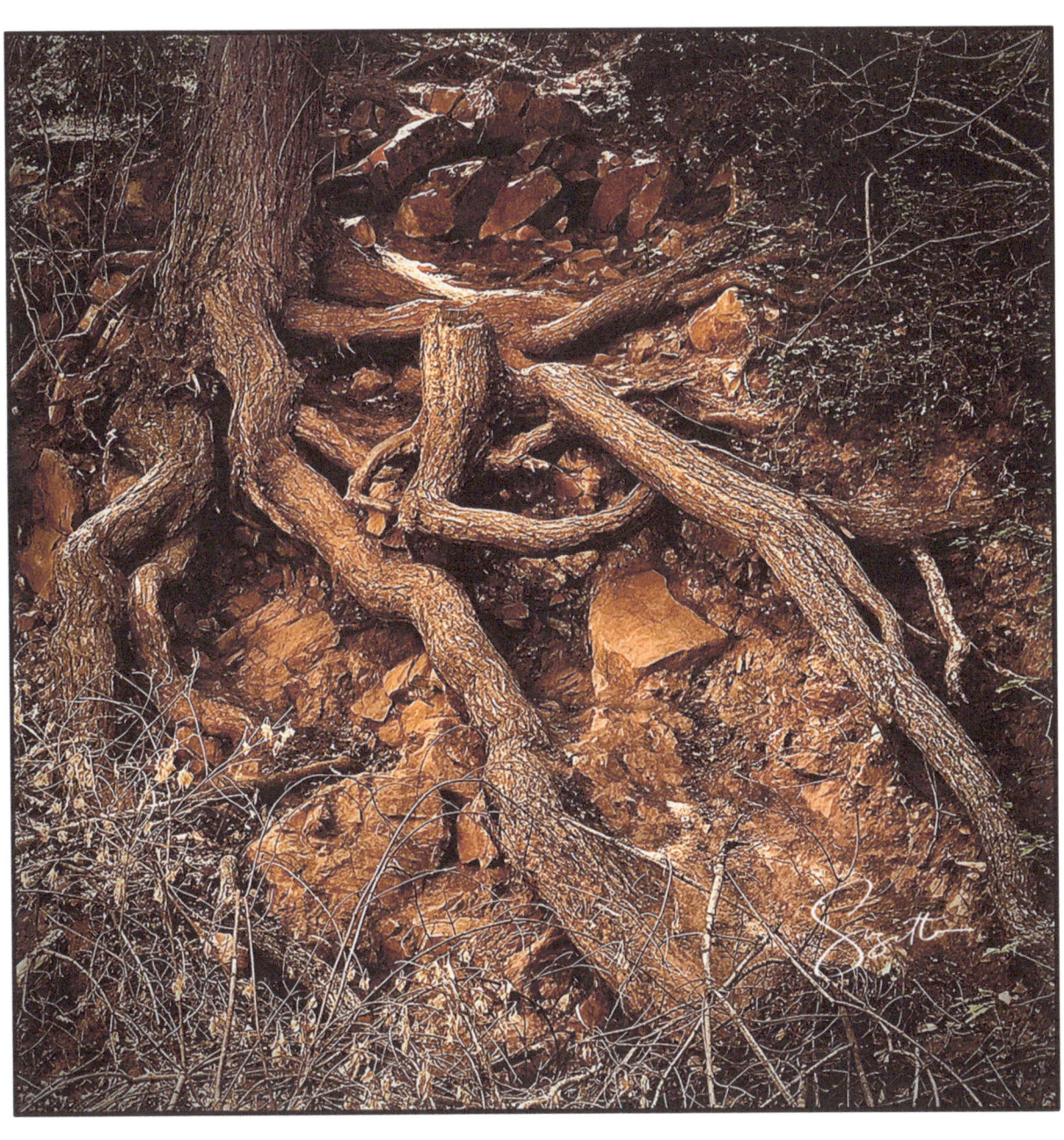

"Look deep into nature, you will understand everything a little better"
~Einstein

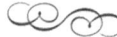

I can't wait to escape on a wild rocky path in the mountains again.

I want to feel the cool breeze on my skin and listen to a serenade of birds.
I want to turn upward and let the sun permeate my entire being.

I want to expand outward into the depths of nature
so I can dive inward and absorb the eternal depths of me.

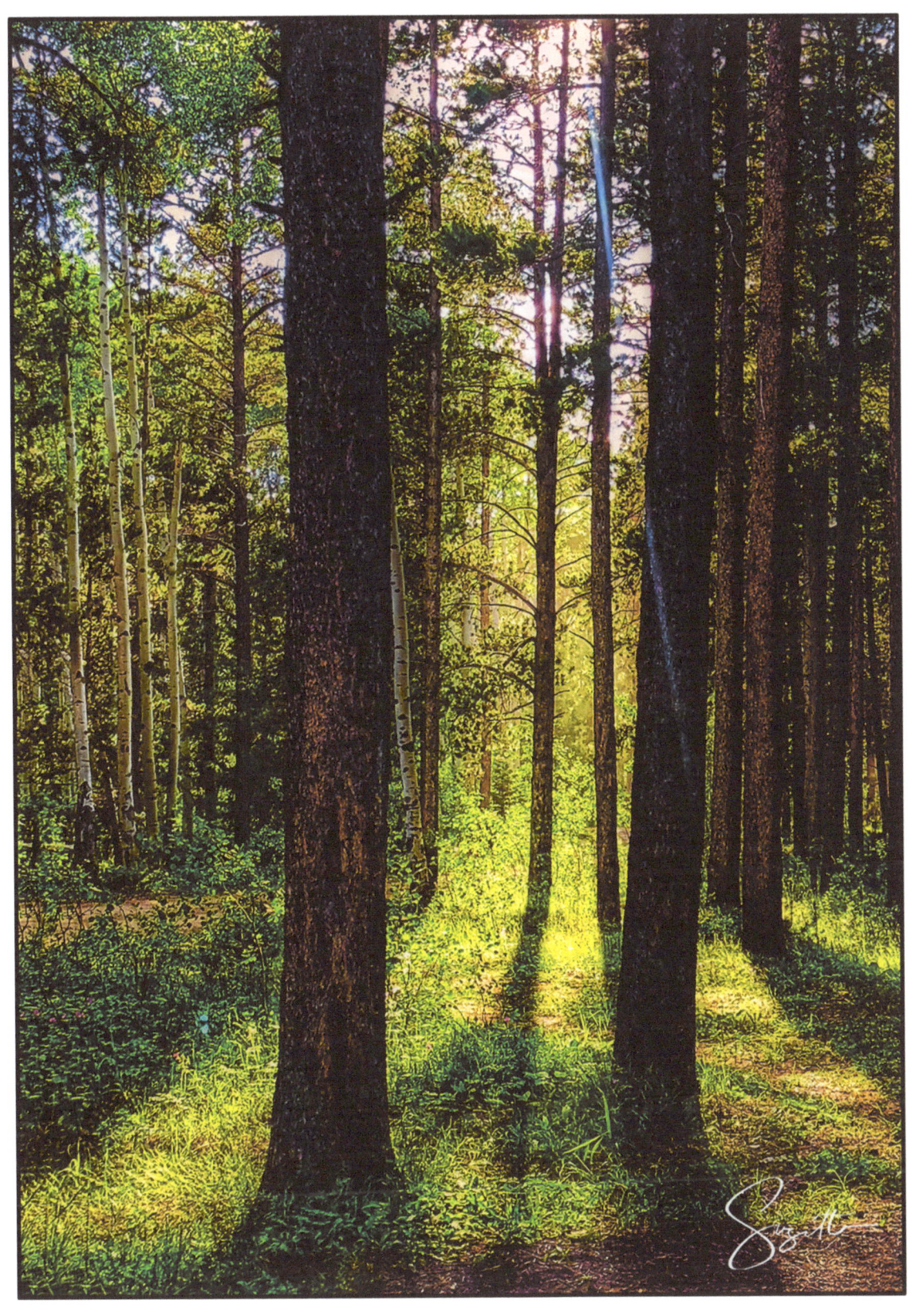

*"Climb the mountains and get their good tidings.
Nature's peace will flow into you as sunshine flows into trees."
~John Muir*

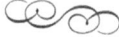

Why do we allow ourselves to get so tangled up with life
that we miss all there is surrounding us?
Uncomplicated and in the moment, all things will be revealed.

Contentment lies in simplicity.

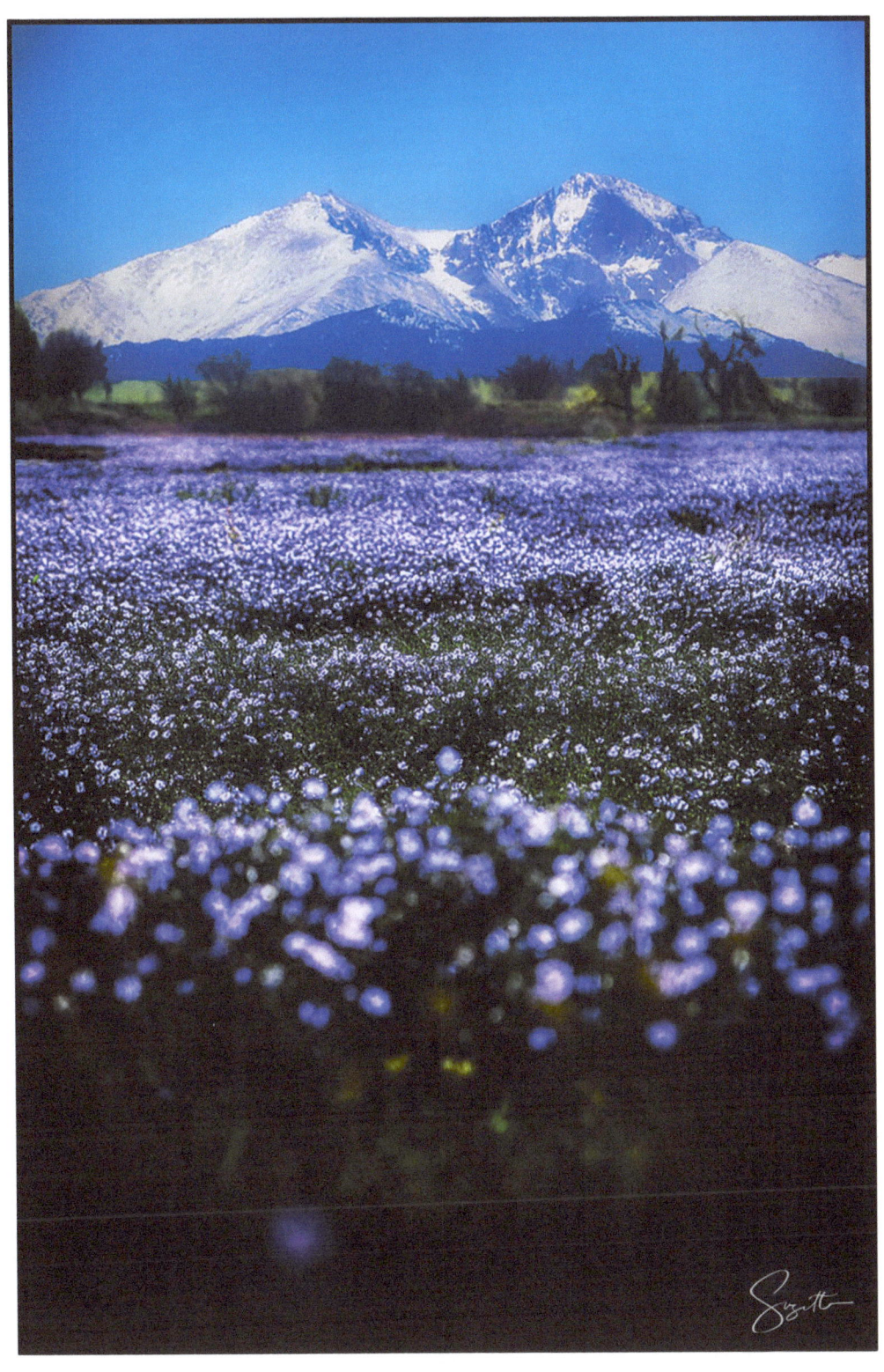

"When you realize there's nothing lacking, the whole world belongs to you".
~ Lao Tzu

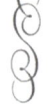

The ever-changing circumstances on earth will always be ever-changing. If you rely on these circumstances, you will also be unbalanced and erratic.

Step inside your Core and become a pillar of strength and consistency.

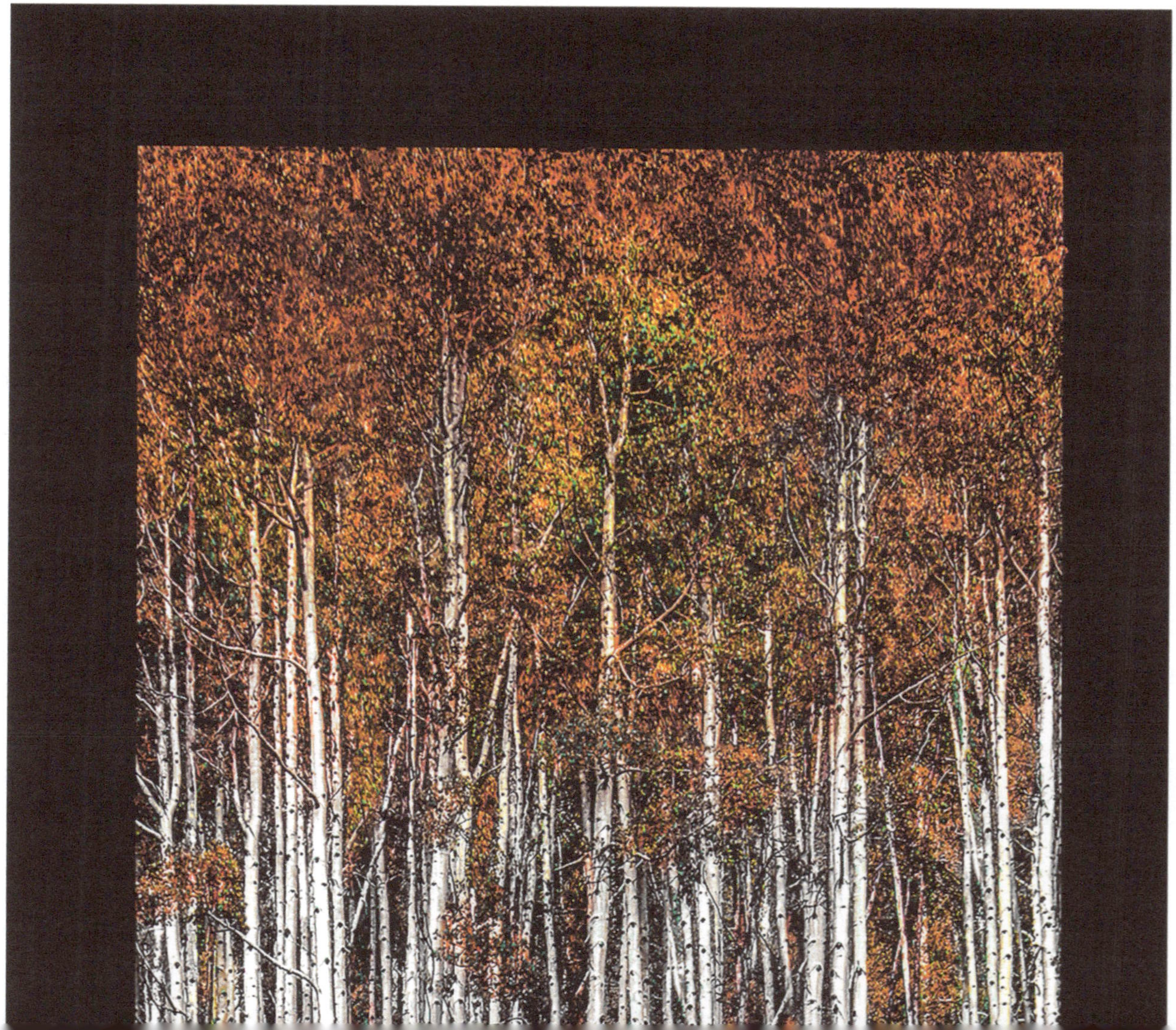

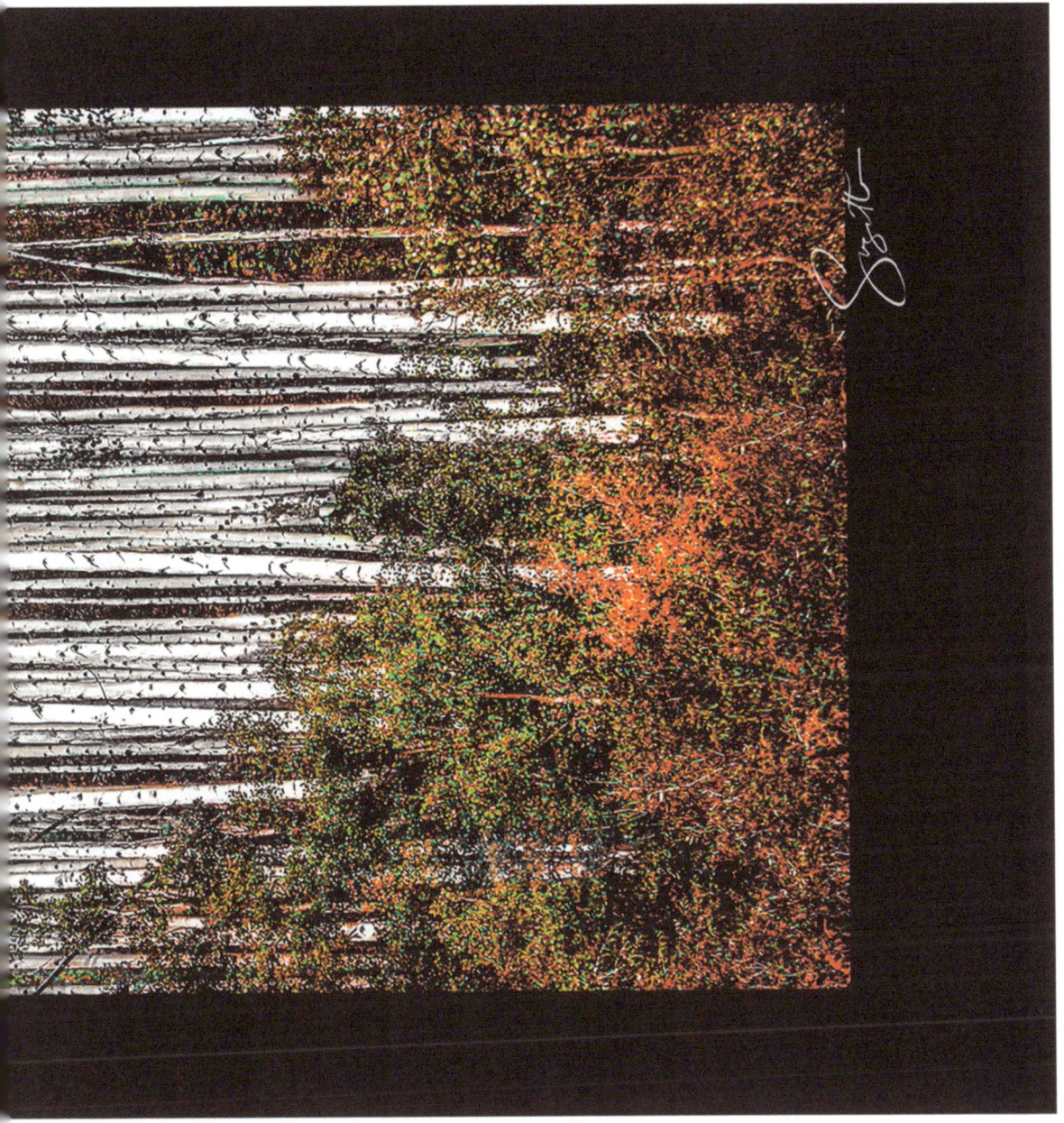

"Trees have the right idea: go deep, branch out, reach high."
~Anita Bondi

I want to believe there's a Greater Power surrounding me and within me,
but the influence of daily existence takes control.
I've been conditioned to see only what's placed before me,
only what I can physically touch.

It's easier that way.
I don't have to look too far for temporary satiation,
but never really experiencing lasting contentment.

The more I take time to step away
and find a place to nurture the Spirit inside me,
the more I can embrace it and take it with me out into everyday life
for endless internal abundance.

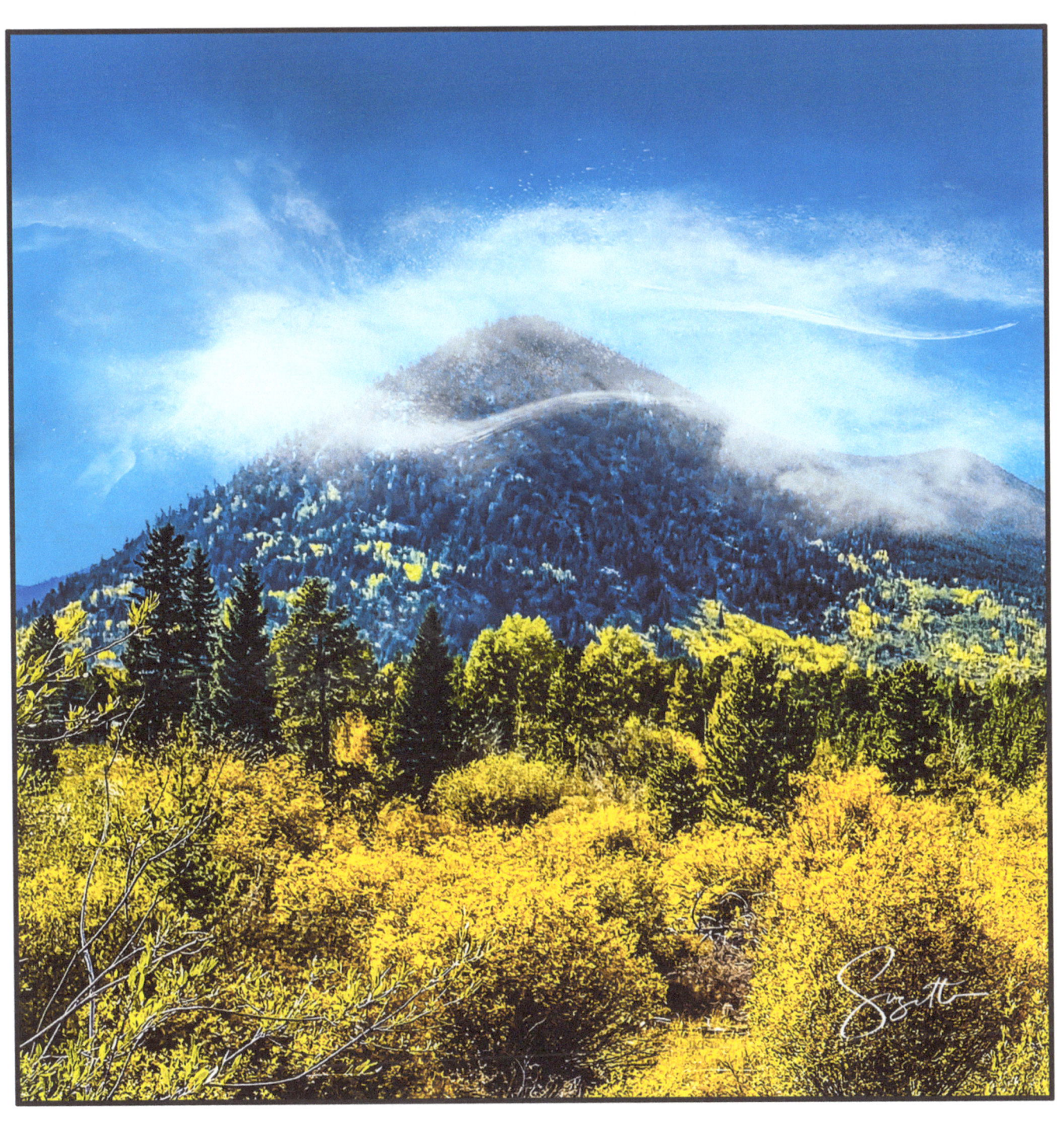

"Nature always wears the colors of the spirit."
~Ralph Waldo Emerson

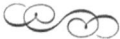

Today I went for a walk in the woods
and waited for the solitude of my Inner Sanctuary to show up,
but then I realized she was there all along —
infiltrating me, surrounding me,
embracing me from within.

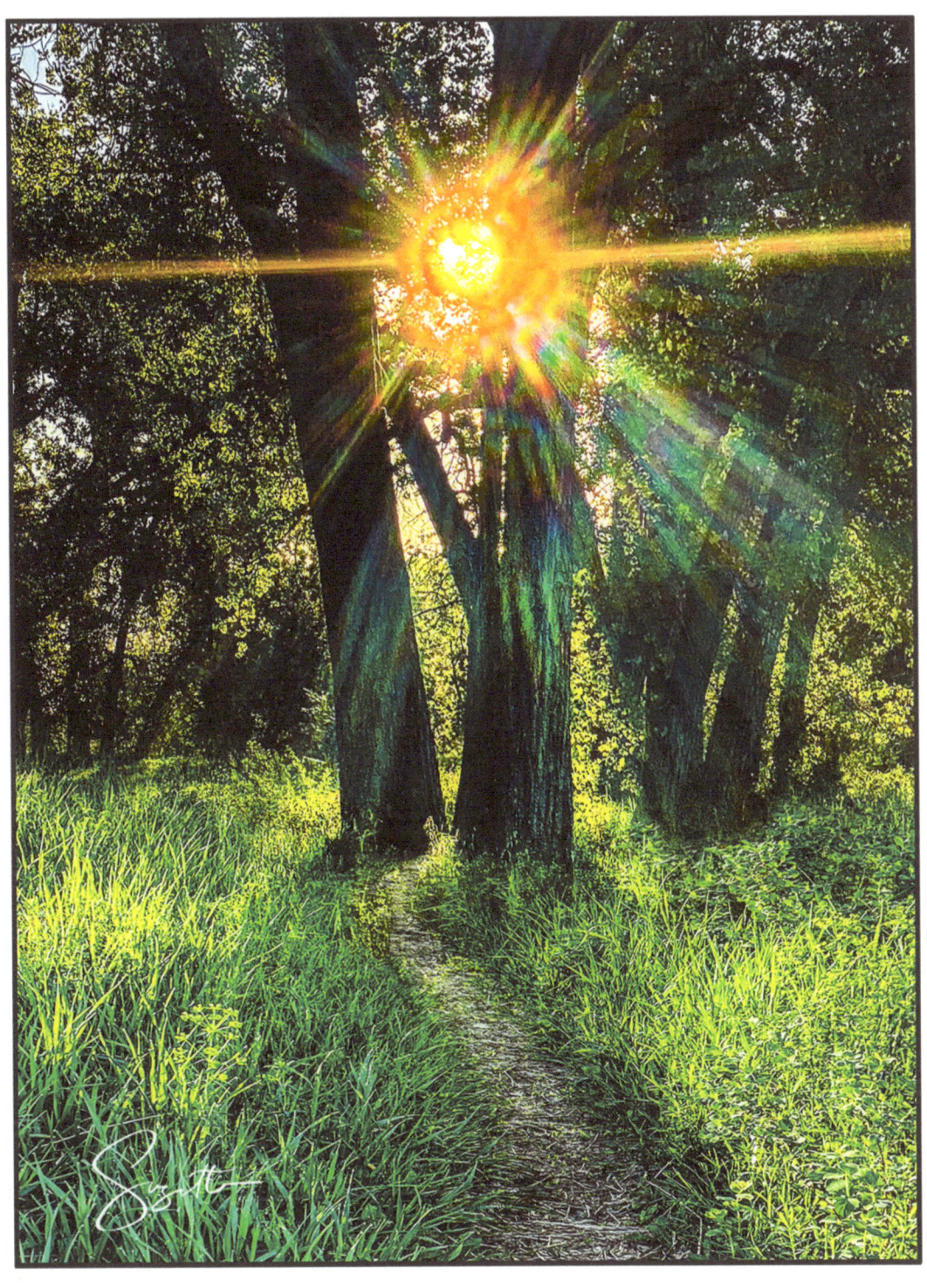

*"I only went out for a walk and finally concluded to stay till sundown
- for going out, I found I was really going in."*
~John Muir

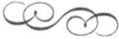

When I've taken time in nature, I feel complete.
But then I return home,
entangle myself back into the complexity of living
and my calm disintegrates.
Tranquility is a mind-shift away at any minute, in any situation.
Stillness lies in your next breath.

Take it with you as you go.

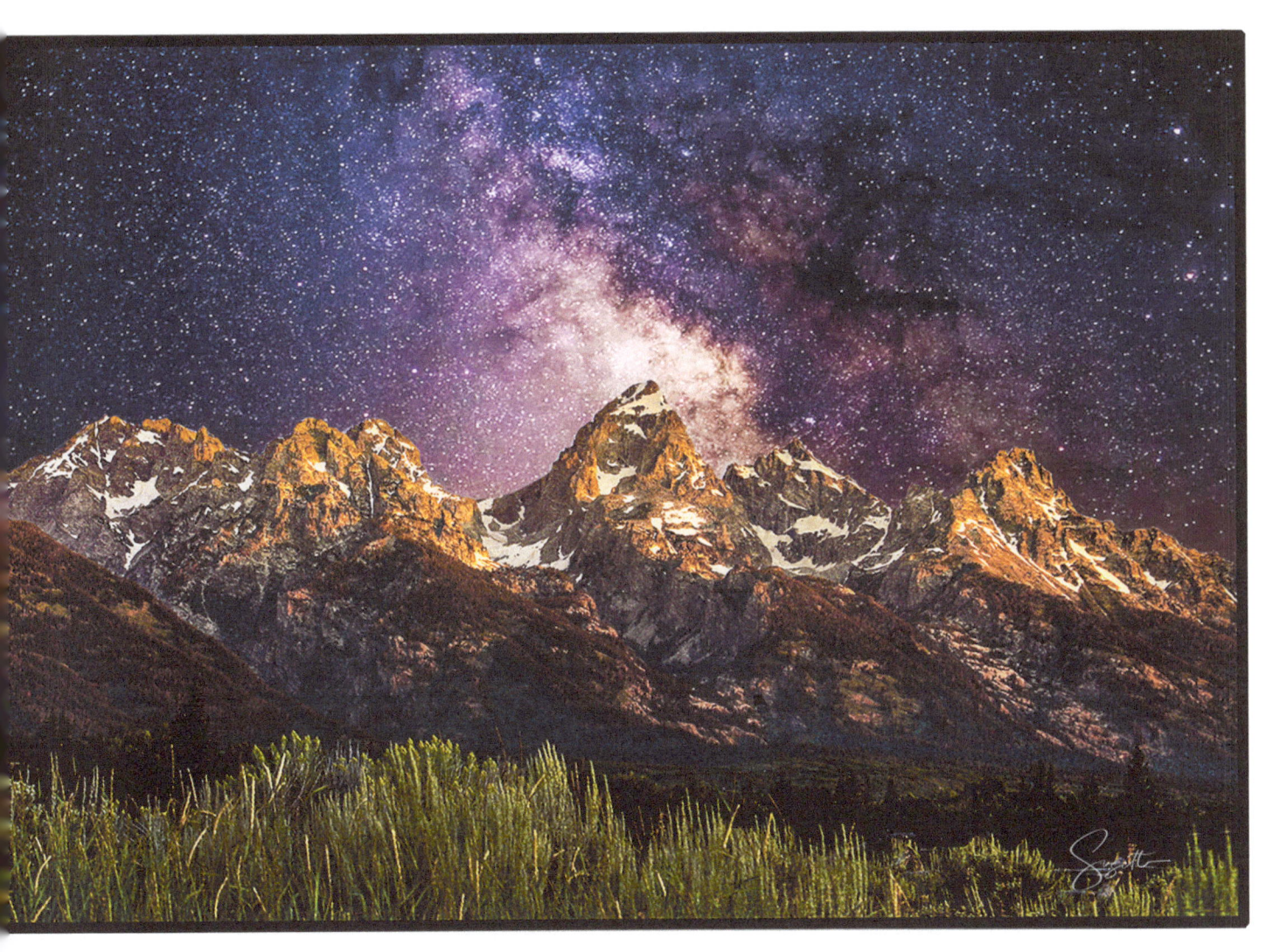

"To the mind that is still, the whole universe surrenders."
~Lao Tzu

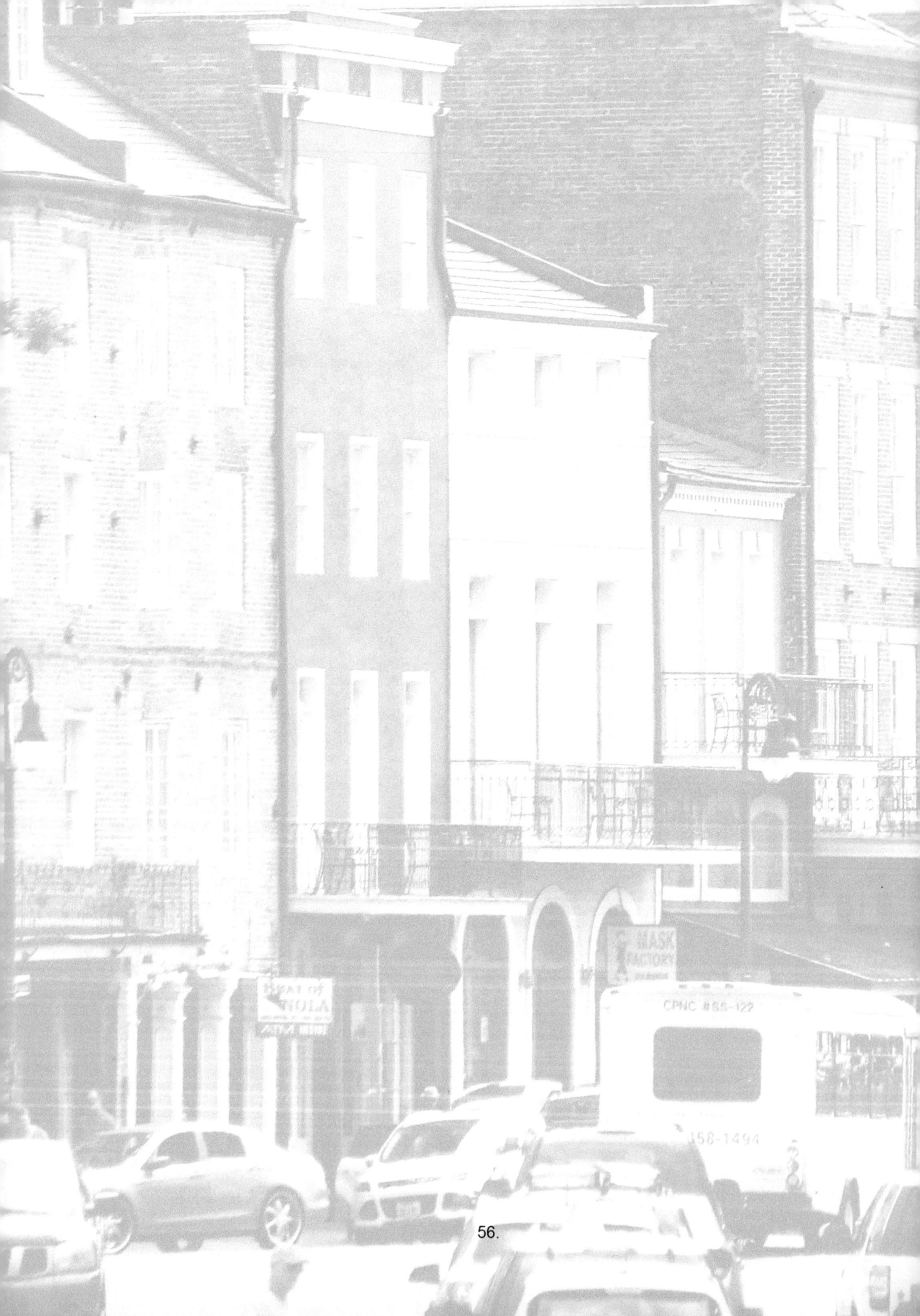

City Streets

Most days are complicated. They can become entangled with distractions, and absorbed with the hustle, the climb.

You can't always have the comfort of nature to bring stillness, but you can practice taking that inner clarity with you as you venture out into the day. With your mind clear from negativity and judgment you can step beyond the chaos and listen.

In the space beyond commotion, there's a detached stillness where you can view the world from all perspectives, seeing where you need to be and hearing what
you need to say.

The art of being alive is embracing stillness in chaos.

"Can you hear the soundless beyond all the noise?"
~Byron Katie

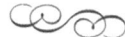

Stress levels, planning, and activity turn awareness away.
Opportunities disintegrate if your mind is occupied.

No matter what's going on in your day,
allow the Spirit within you to flow.

Listen.

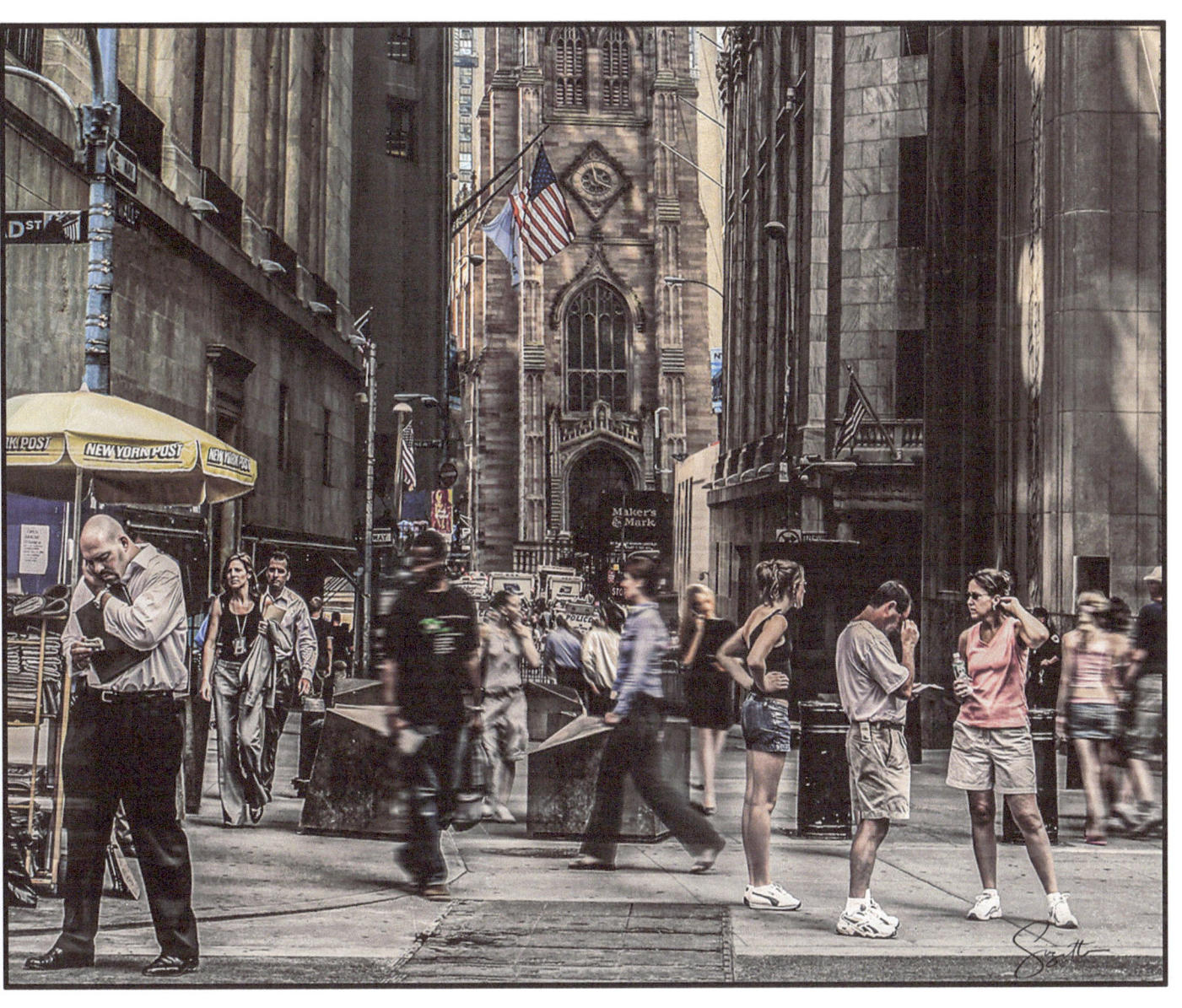

"Life is something that happens to you while you're making other plans"
~Margaret Millar

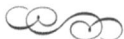

I wake up every morning with the best of intentions,
but then the day begins:
an unexpected phone call, the driver with road rage, long lines, running late, traffic.

Daily influences dilute who I am and what I came here to do.
Daily influences steal today's beauty.

Remembering Goethe's quote gives me a slight shift of mindset
and reminds me that today is all there is.

Nothing is worth more than this day.

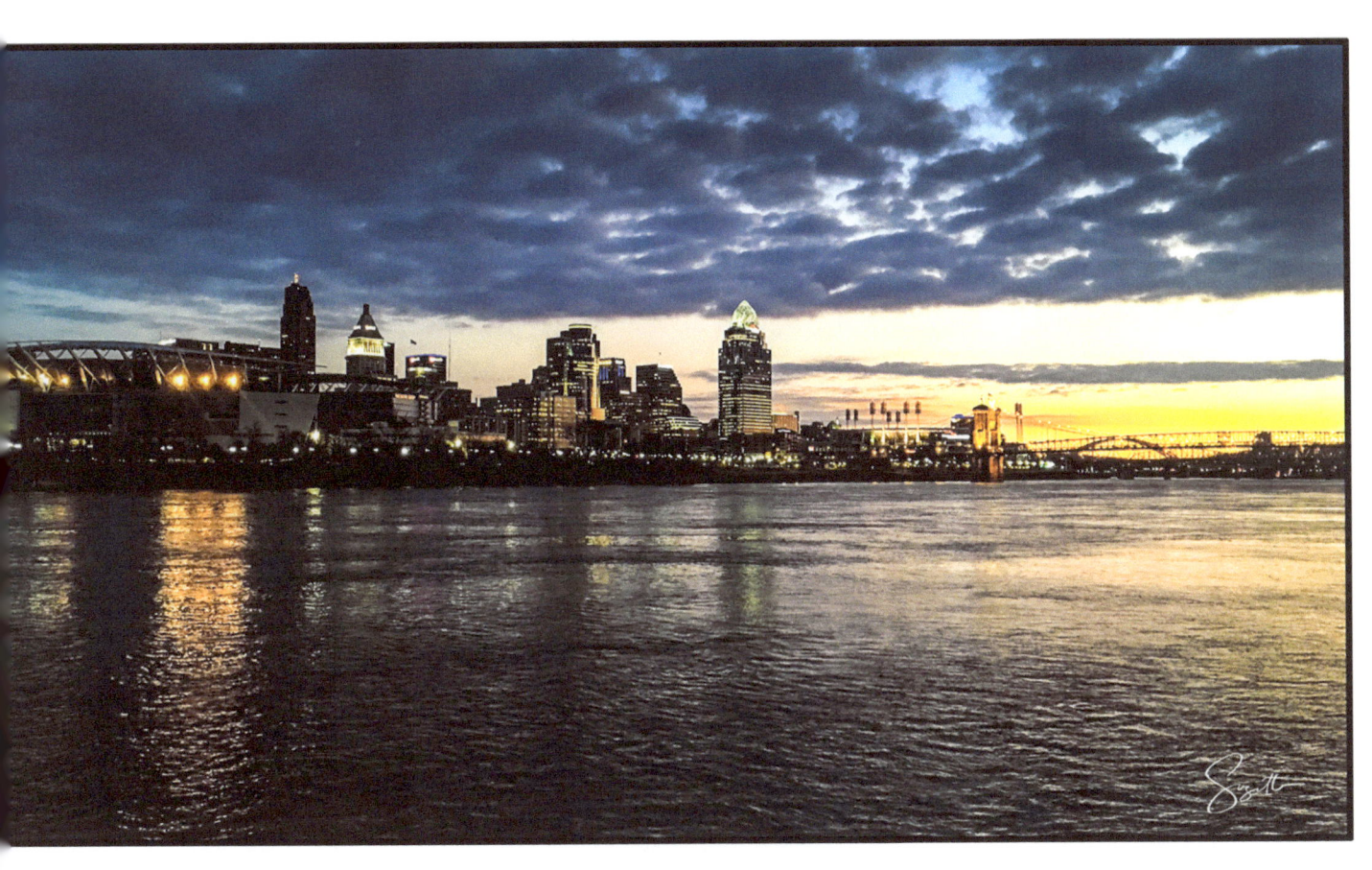

"Nothing is worth more than this day."
~Goethe

Noise is all around;
but instead of reaching inward to the comfort of your inner sanctuary,
the commotion causes an irritating, outward focus.

Connect to the clamor, or align with the flow of energy from within.
It's your choice every minute of the day.

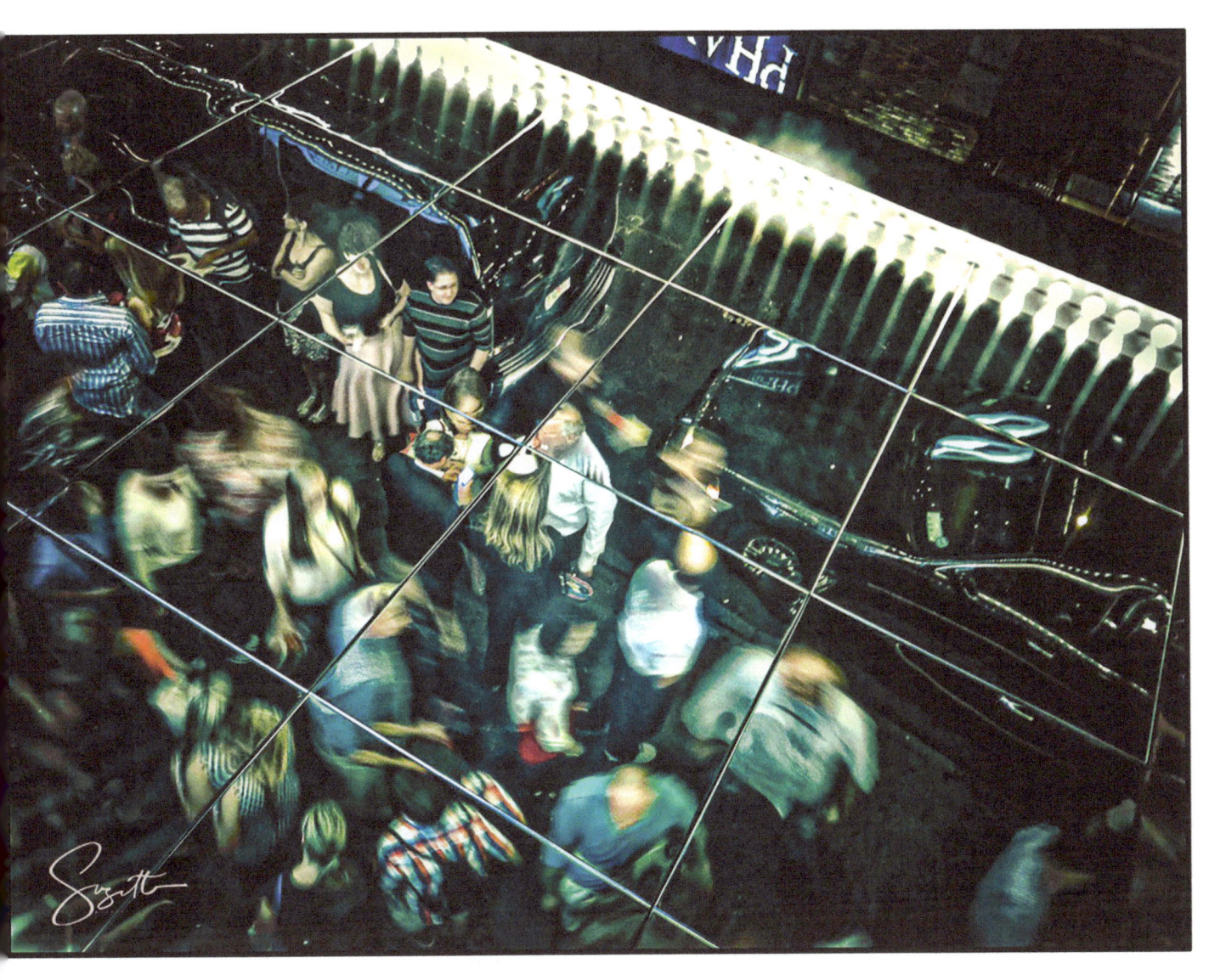

"There's going to be stress in life,
but it's your choice whether you let it affect you or not."
~Valerie Bertinelli

When I was in the mandated 'lockdown' during the 2020 pandemic,
I was able to see life from a different perspective behind closed doors.

It was then that I realized the things I've been chasing
are not as important as I thought.

Without those 'things' out there to chase,
I had space to breathe
and space to think
and space to embrace the screaming 'me' within.

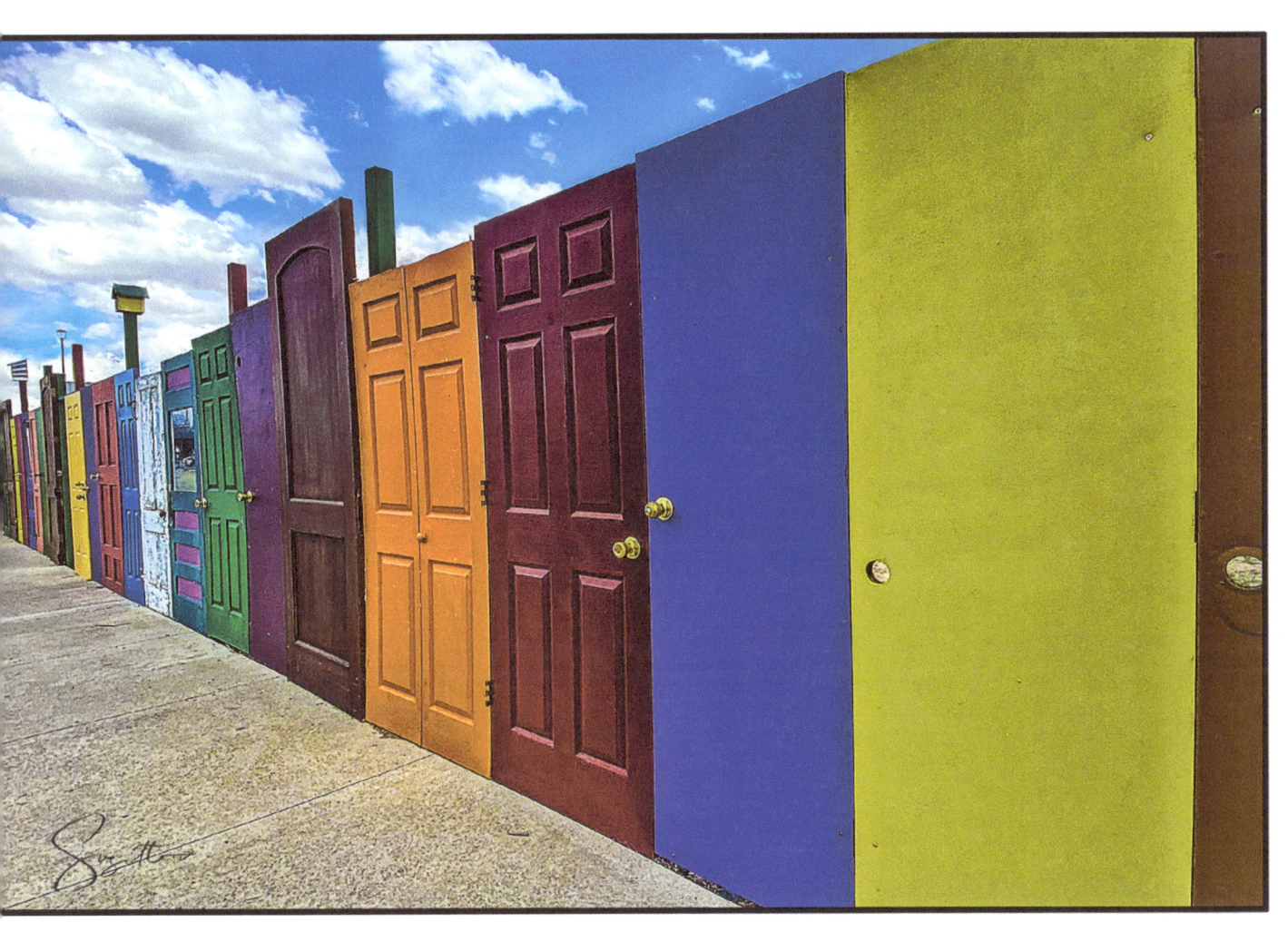

"What I am searching for is not out there, it is in me"
~ Helen Keller

There's always so much to get done in a day:
The lists, the deadlines, the pressures.

Stop for a minute and experience where you are right now,
this moment in time.

...Breathe...

Can you feel the silence?
A brief quieting of the mind.

Imagine if you took this internal silence
back out into the rest of your day.

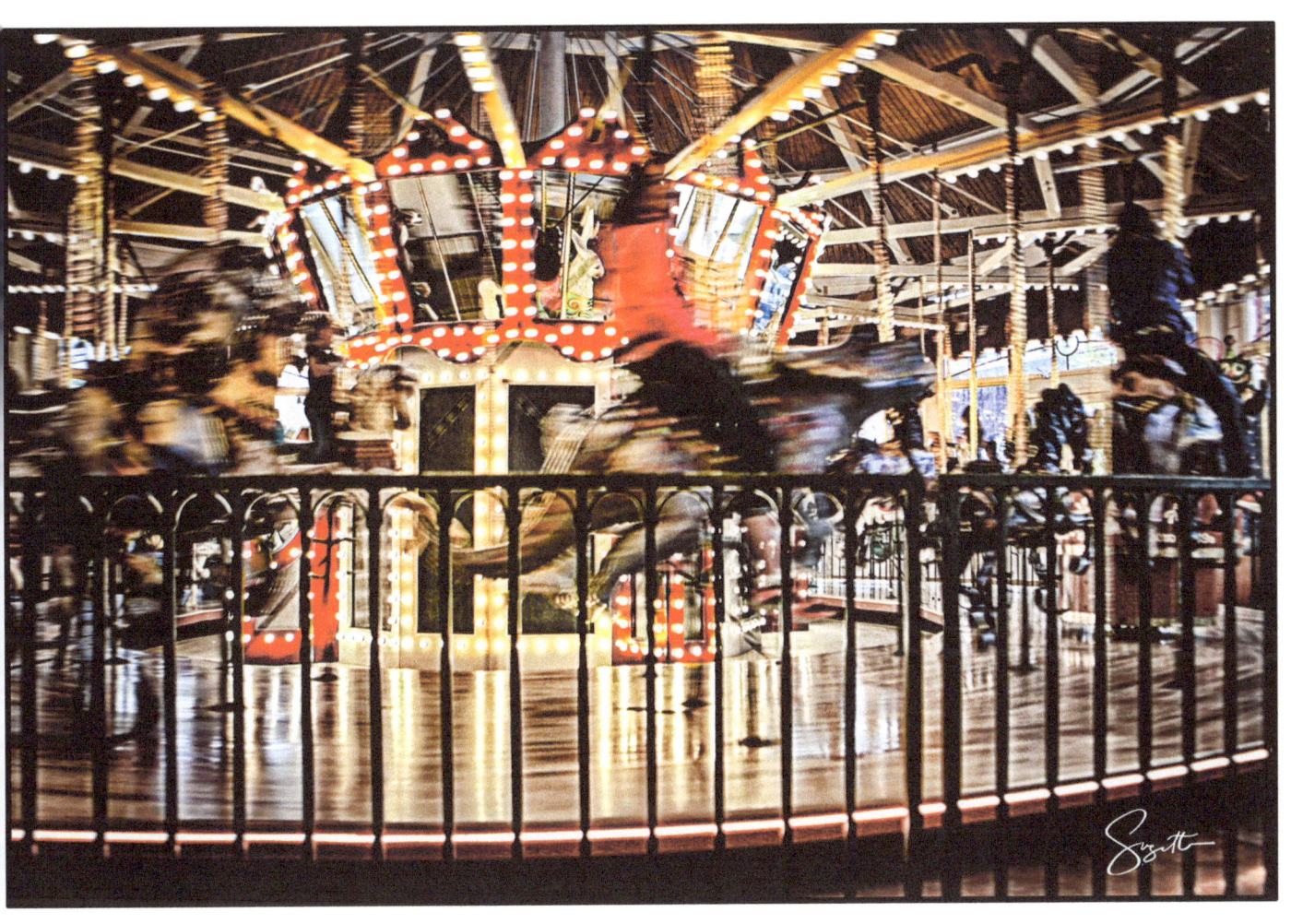

"One of the greatest attacks of the enemy is to make you so busy there is no room for silence."
  ~ Paul Washero

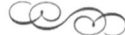

We fight stillness.

There are a thousand other things that need to be done to
'earn the right' to daream and speculate. Even now as I write,
my mind can easily drift to something else I should be doing.

Solitude and introspection are ours for the taking any minute of
the day by simply tuning in and allowing the space to slow down around
us.

It's then that profound insights emerge.

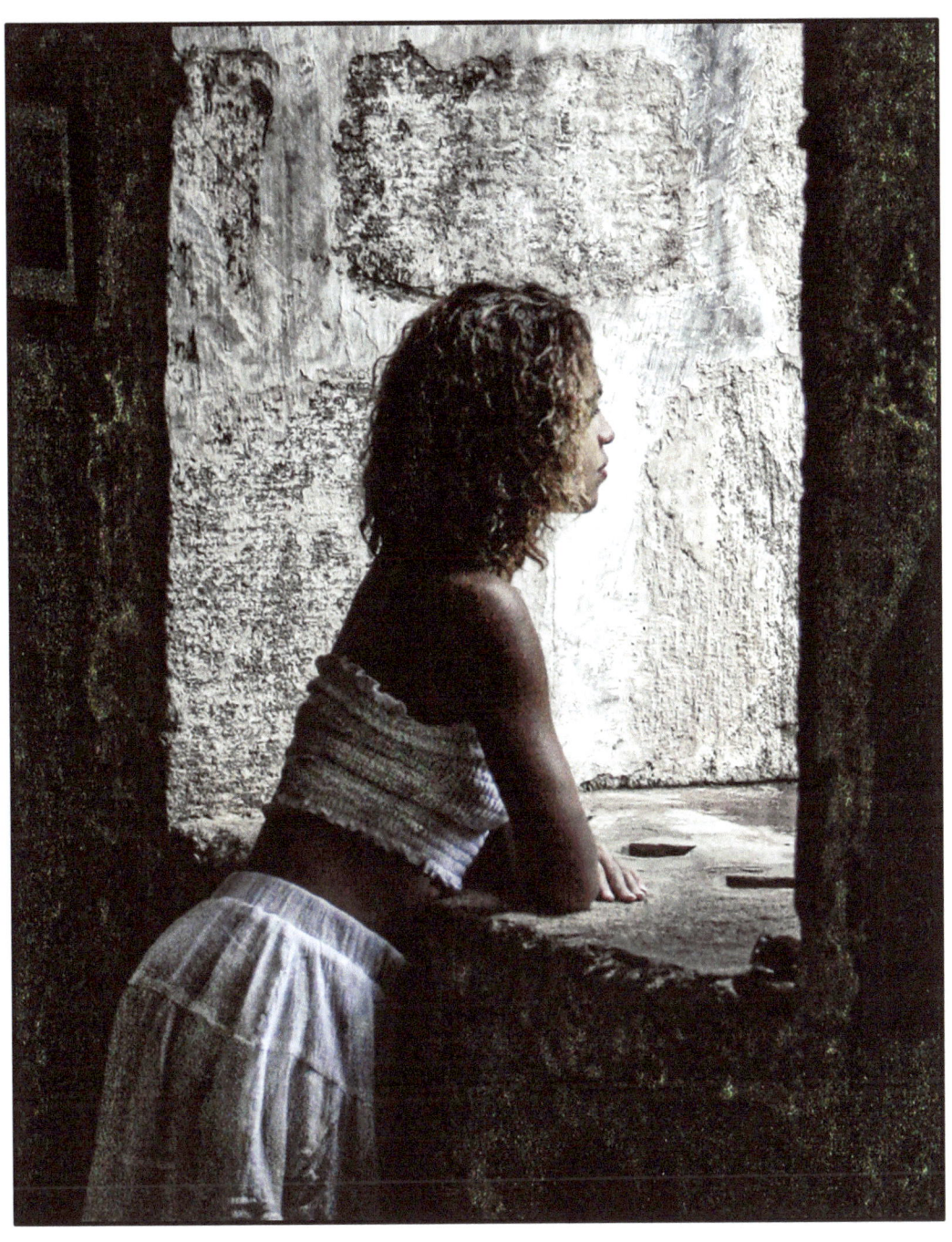

"Allow yourself permission to dream."
~ Randy Paush

More times than I care to admit during a day
I allow my mind to race into the discomfort of what I 'should' to be doing.
Inspiration dissolves as stillness spirals into tension.

This disconnect from the calm of internal focus is much easier.
It takes less work.
I simply tap into the external
and allow whatever comes into my path control my emotions.

It takes more work to move inward and listen,
but when I'm there, the tension from the external pressure slides away
and I can relax into who I am.

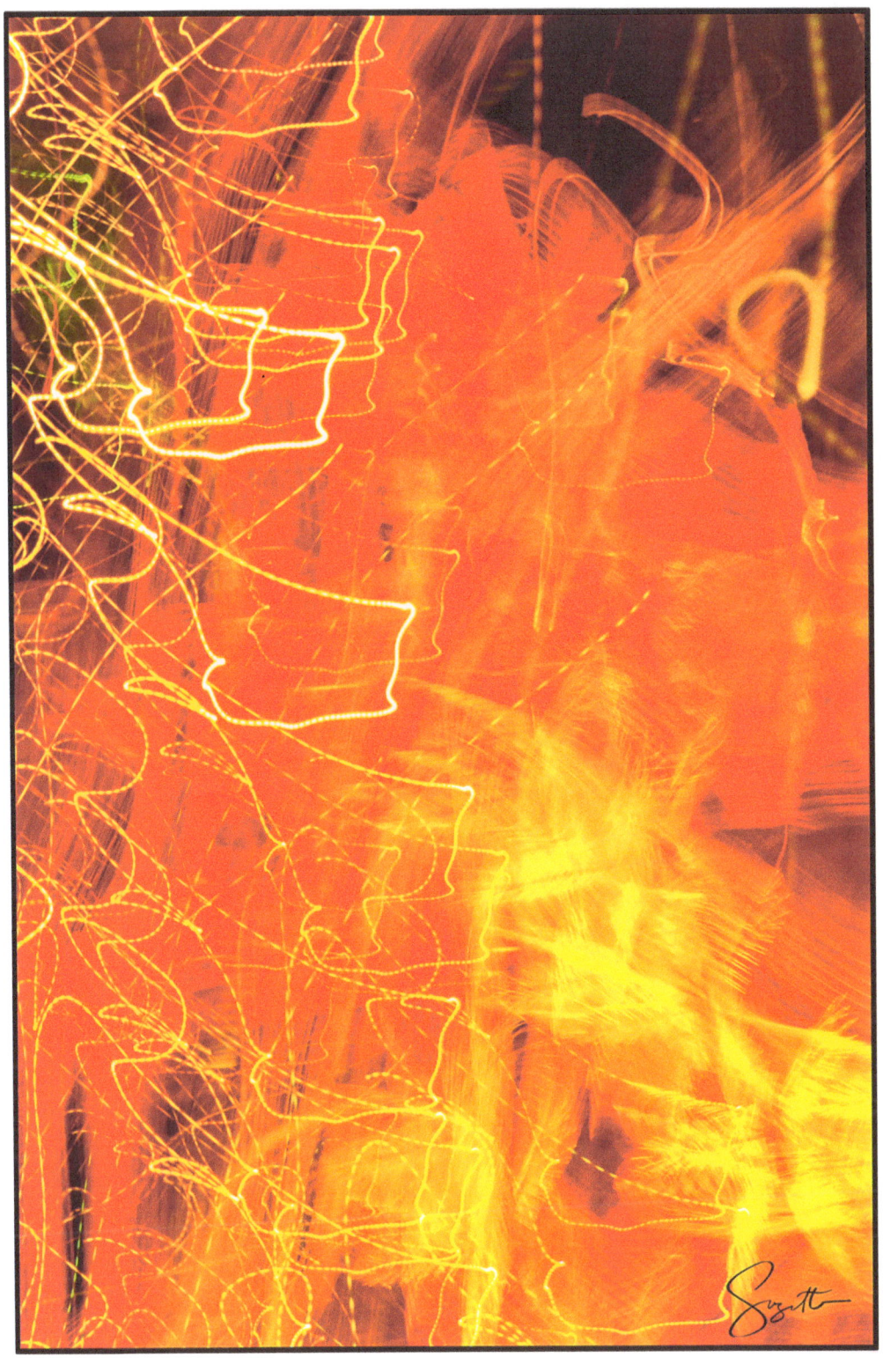

"Tension is who you think you should be, relaxation is who you are."
~Chinese proverb

What is this abstract entity known as 'soul'? What do you think about the idea that 'soul' is a place that functions outside of time, a place for realization and a place where answers come clearly and freely?

There are volumes of answers out there about anything you want to know, but learning about the soul requires opening up to the flow within. The flow that whispers perception, brilliance, and wisdom.

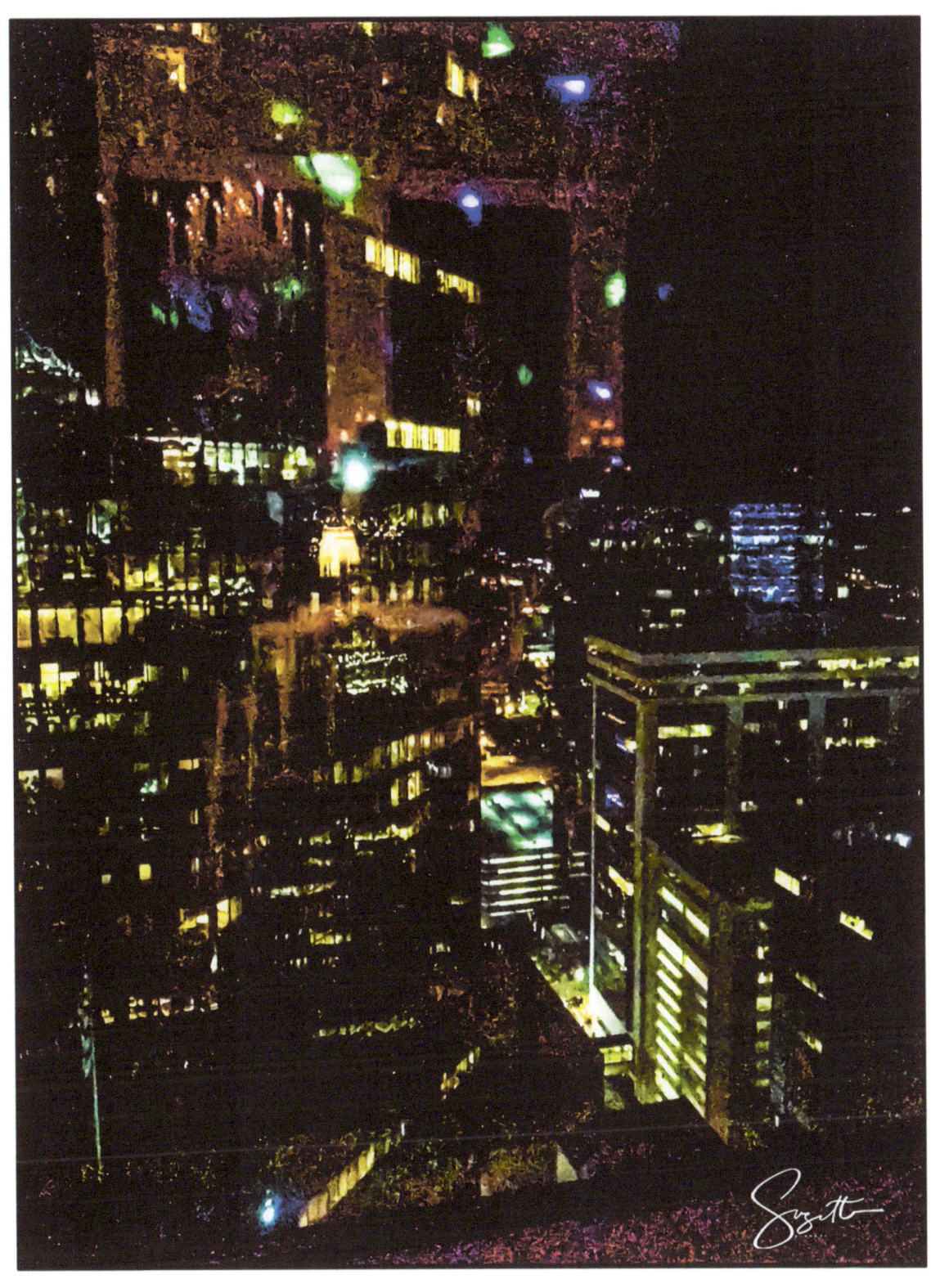

"Four thousand volumes of metaphysics will not teach us what the soul is."
~Voltaire

Next time you're feeling unsettled, journey inward.
Find some solitude.
It's like momentarily turning down the volume of the world.
Find comfort in the chaos.

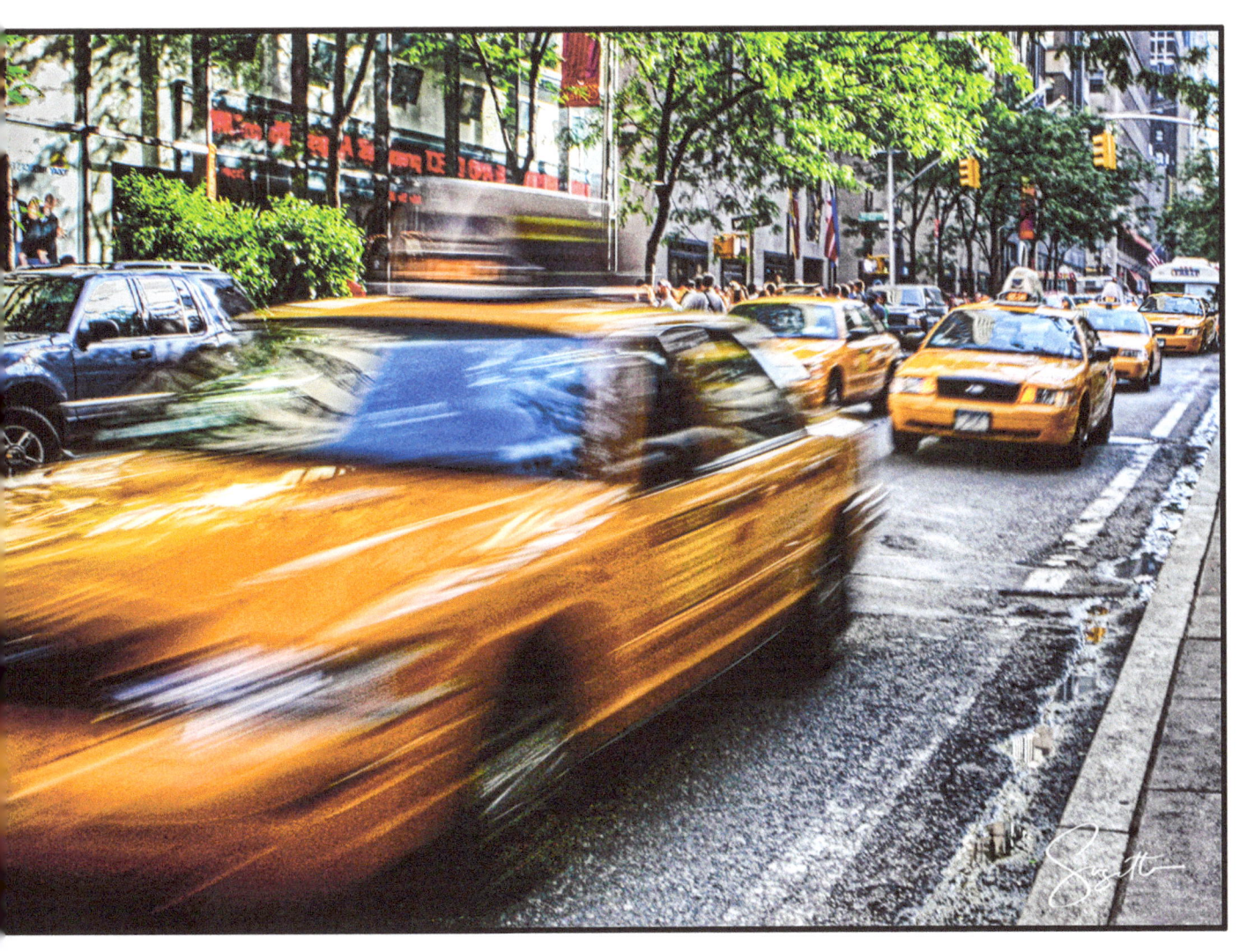

"Days are chaotic. In the noisy confusion, stillness lies within."
~Suzette

There's a constant tug of war between heaven and hell within.

It's easy to allow the negative.
It takes a mindless effort to let it seep in and take over.
Your beautiful soul is merely a guest sharing space with this damaging influence.

We can't fight this battle alone.
Allow the strength of a Greater Power to move inside and win the battle for you.
You can then rise above into the luscious levels of contentment, peace, and comfort.

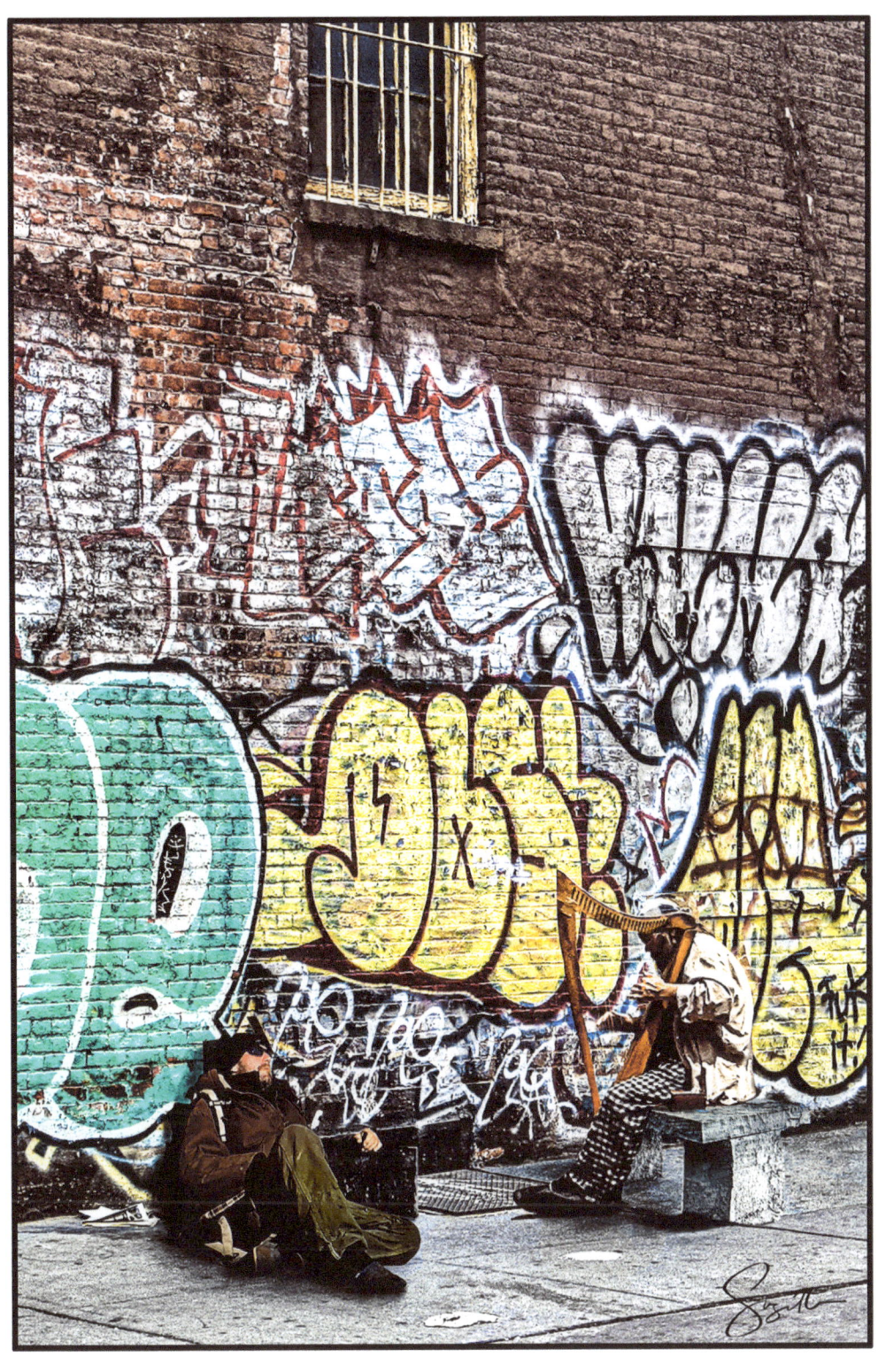

"To different minds, the same world is a hell, and a heaven."
~ Ralph Waldo Emerson

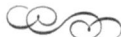

Without the stillness of your Inner Sanctuary
you are more blind than when darkness shields your sight.

Your Source lies amidst the commotion,
but you cannot see it.

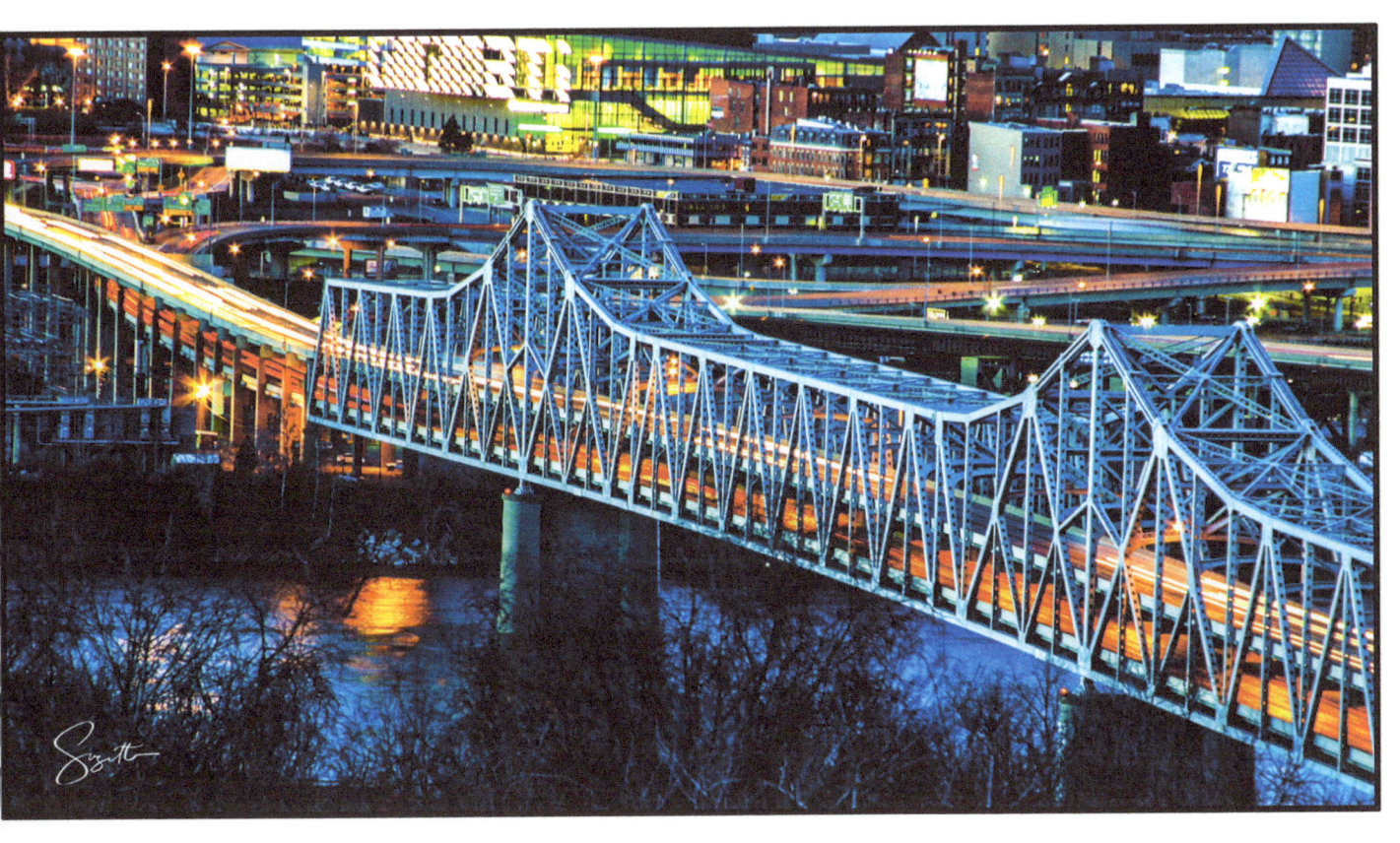

"We need to find God, and he cannot be found in noise and restlessness."
~Mother Teresa

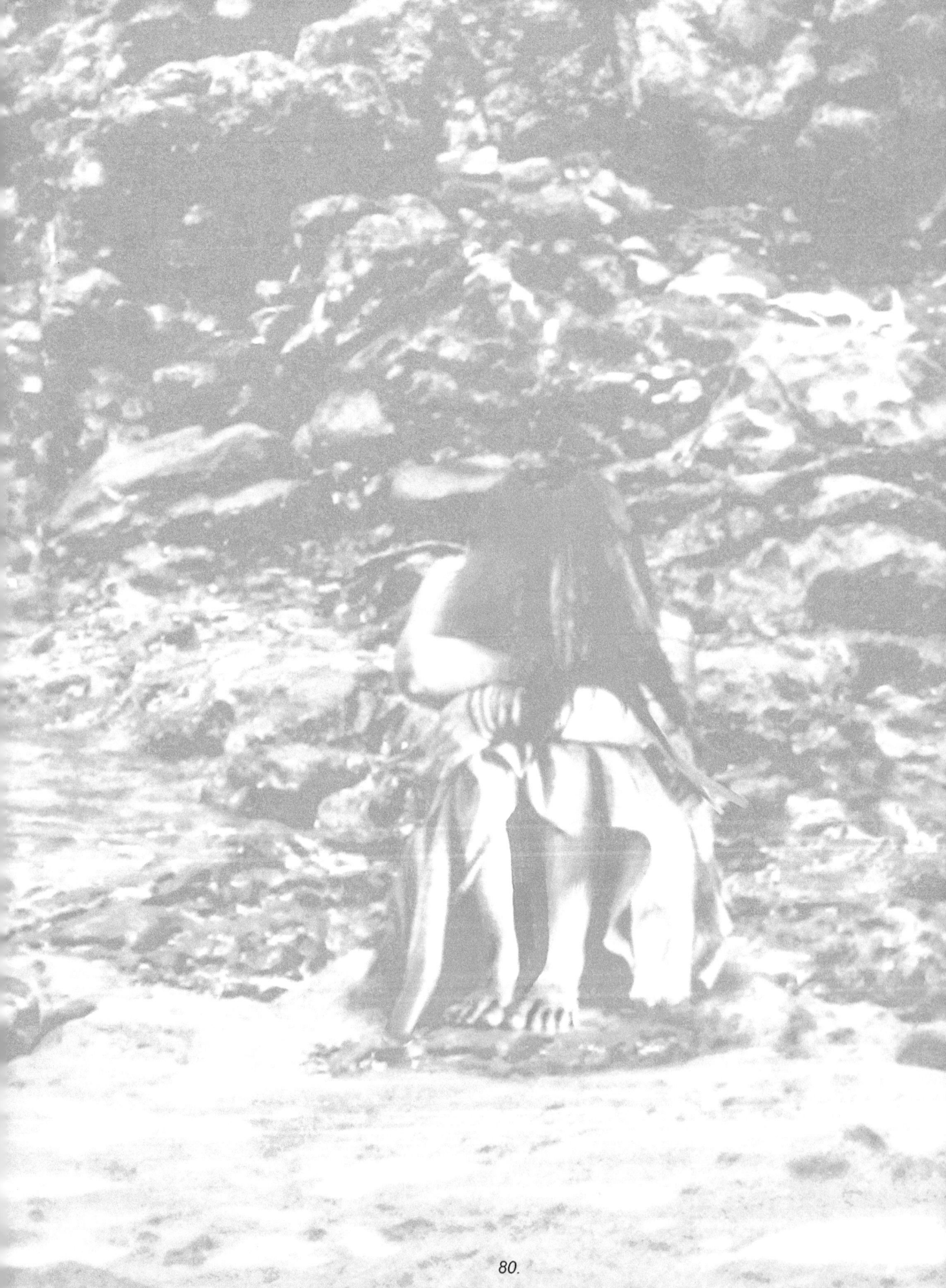

Misfit

After you've let go of some things holding you back and etched the stillness of nature within you, beauty is everywhere – it's in the neglected, the misfit, and even in struggles.

A receptive mind is freeing. It creates the ability to look more meaningfully at the world and at situations happening around you. It magnifies life.

We can move through the day with less judgment, seeing richness in everything.

The art of being alive is savoring beauty in all things.

"There is nothing either good or bad but thinking makes it so."
~Shakespeare

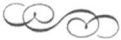

There's magnificence surrounding you every minute of the day
but so much is missed through the congestion of noisy thought.

Noticing beauty is a frame of mind,
and can be accessed by merely stepping into
the awareness of the concept.

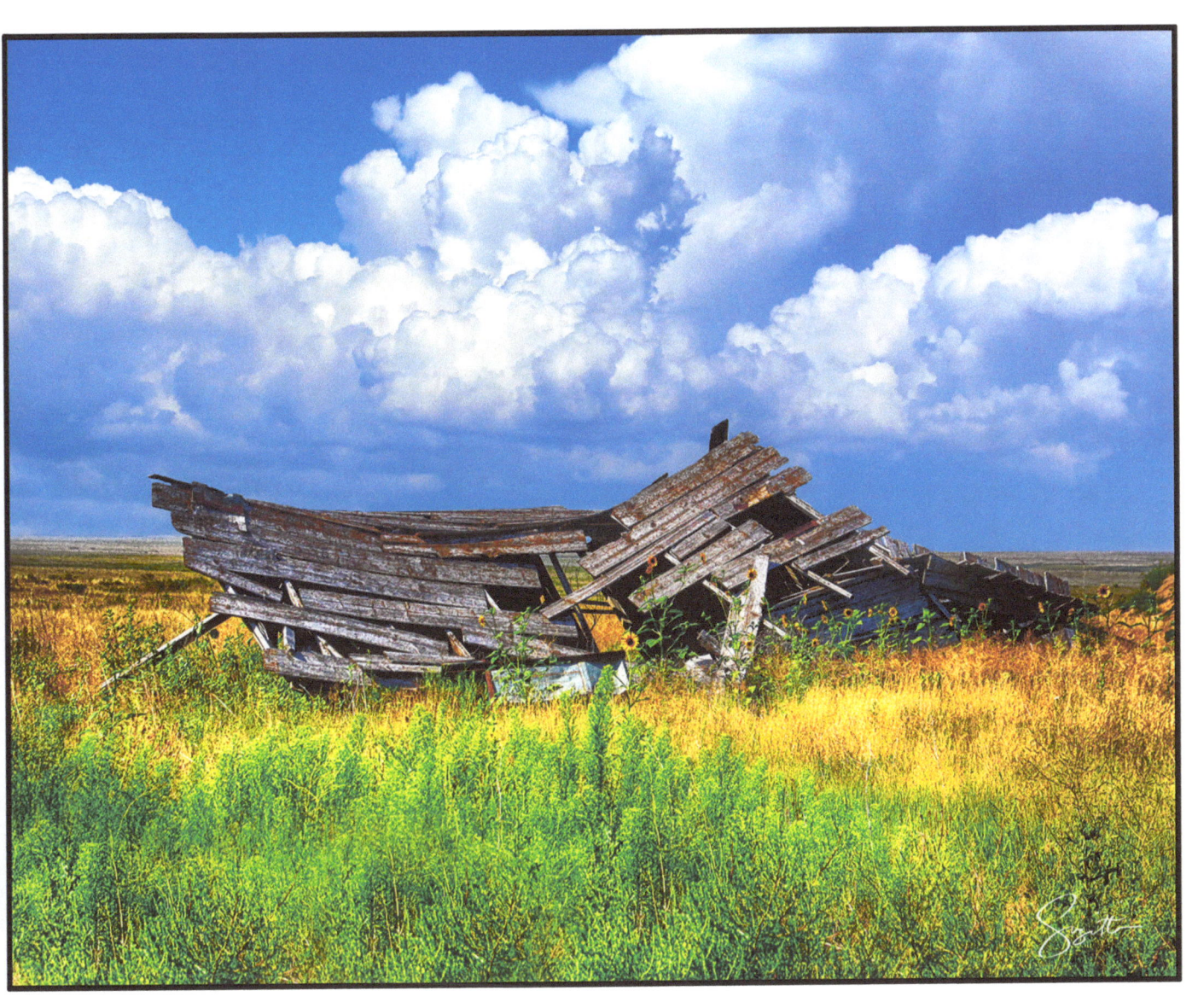

"There are always flowers for those who want to see them."
~Matisse

∽∞

Now, this is one ugly bird;
But this ugly bird won 'Best of Show' a couple of years ago in a print competition.

What makes something worthy of applause?
What draws our attention as we go through the day?

Circumstances are happening around us every minute, both good and bad,
and it's how we choose to see those circumstances that will make the difference.

Ugly or beautiful?
A slight mind-shift makes every encounter extraordinary.

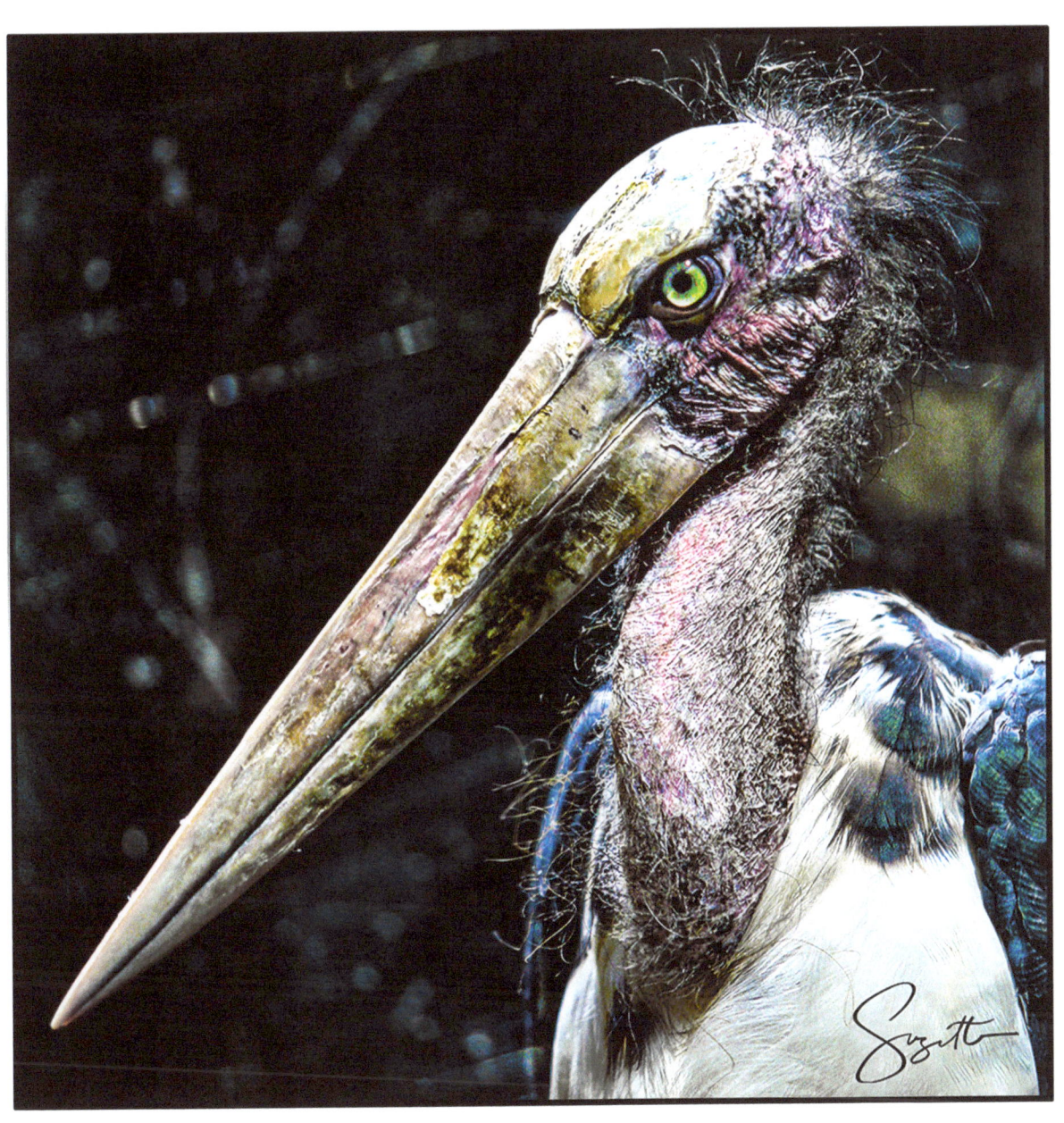

"It's not what you look at that matters, it's what you see."
~ Thoreau

What do you say when you talk to yourself?
If you're like me, I find myself harsher than I need to be.
Imagine saying some of those things to a child.
How confident would the child be
with that kind of language day after day?

Gentleness. Encouragement. Love.
We crave it as any child would.

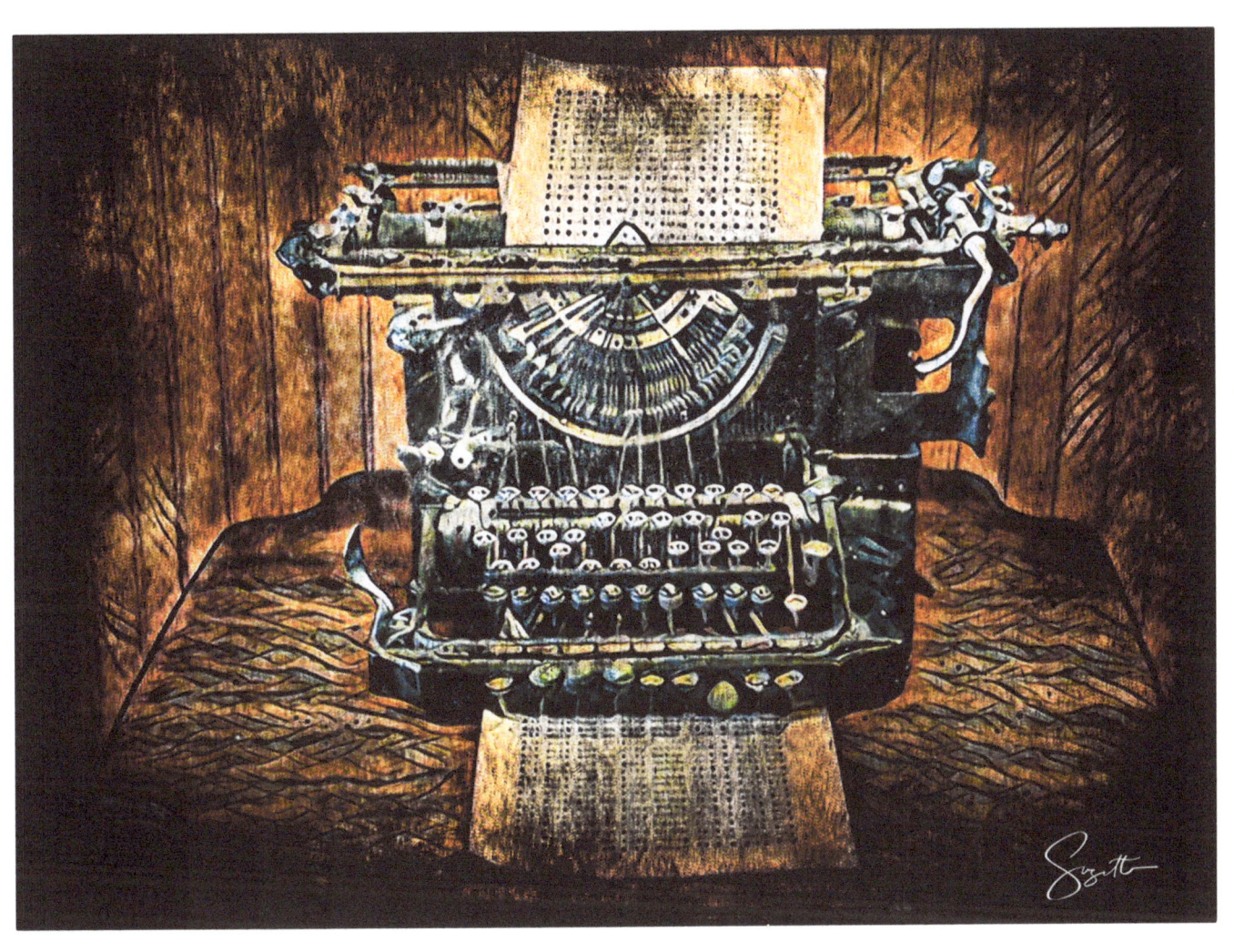

"Talk to yourself like you would talk to someone you love."
~Brene Brown

"Why is everyone so happy here except me?"

"Because they have learned to see goodness and beauty everywhere."
Said the Master.

"Why don't I see goodness and beauty everywhere?"

"Because you cannot see outside of you what you fail to see inside."

~Anthony de Mello

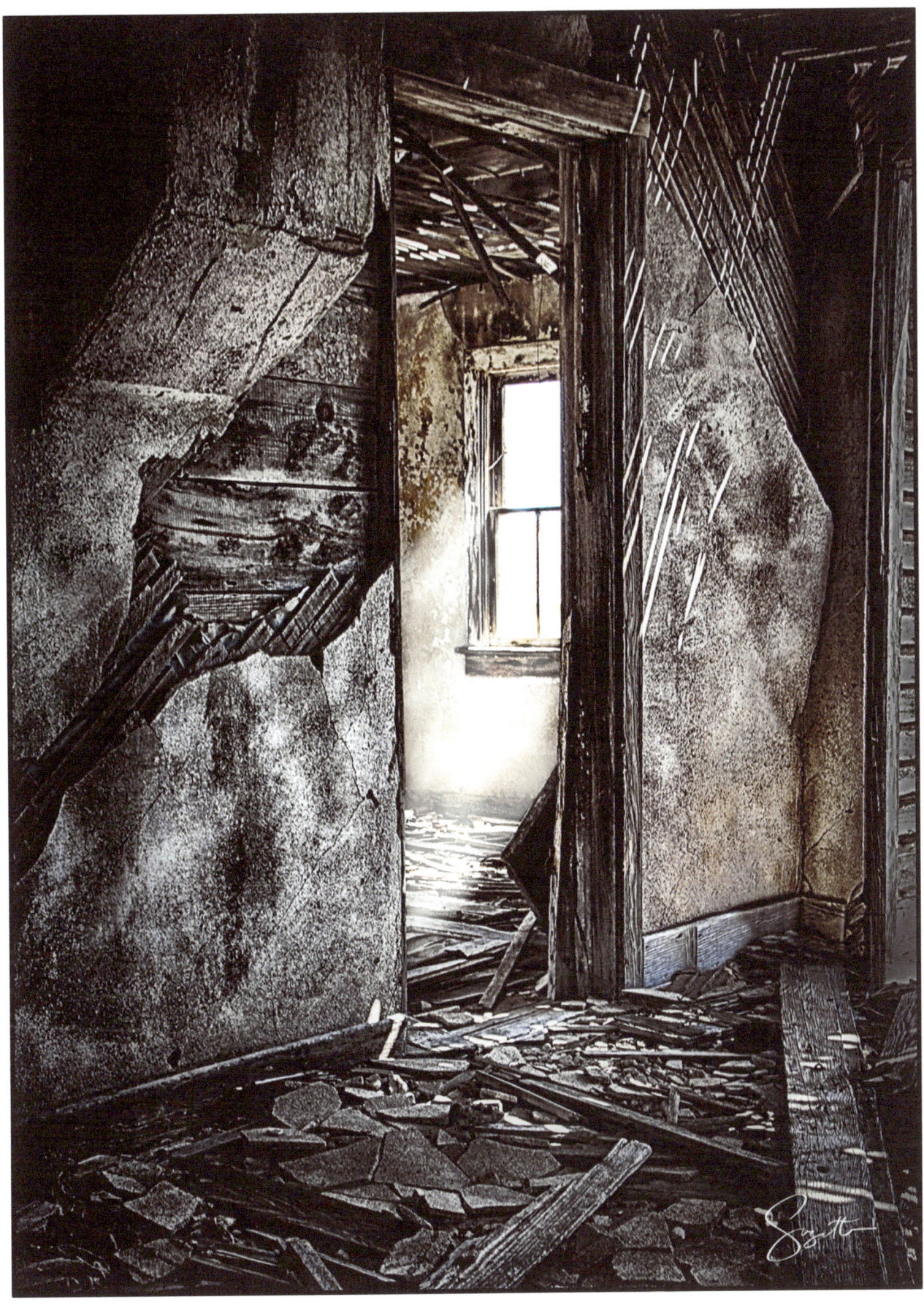

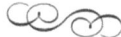

You fear what others think and worry about how they feel. These fears cause blockage, so you can't be all that you can be.

This pain exists because we reach out before reaching in, leaving our souls crying for attention.

Move inward to the Spirit within before you move outward to the world.

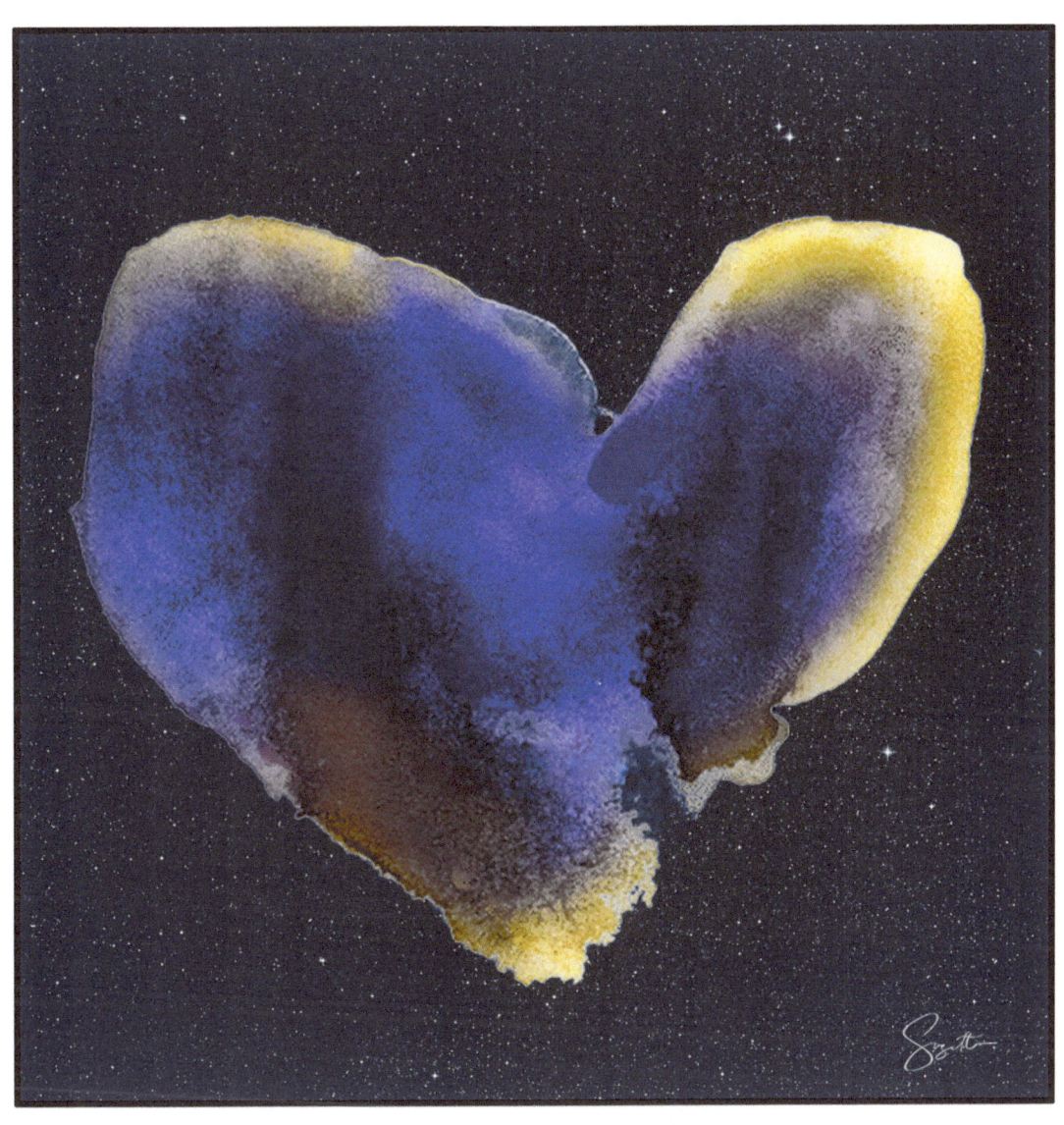

"For Direction, look within."
~the Universe

How do we better see the world?

As a *photographer*, the more I become aware of my surroundings, the more I see.
Observation allows me the opportunity to capture moments
and simplify the world for you as a viewer.

As a *human*, the more I become aware of my surroundings, the more I see.
Observation as a human gives me insight into life around me –
hearing what I need to hear, seeing what I need to see, acting when I need to act,
being where I need to be.

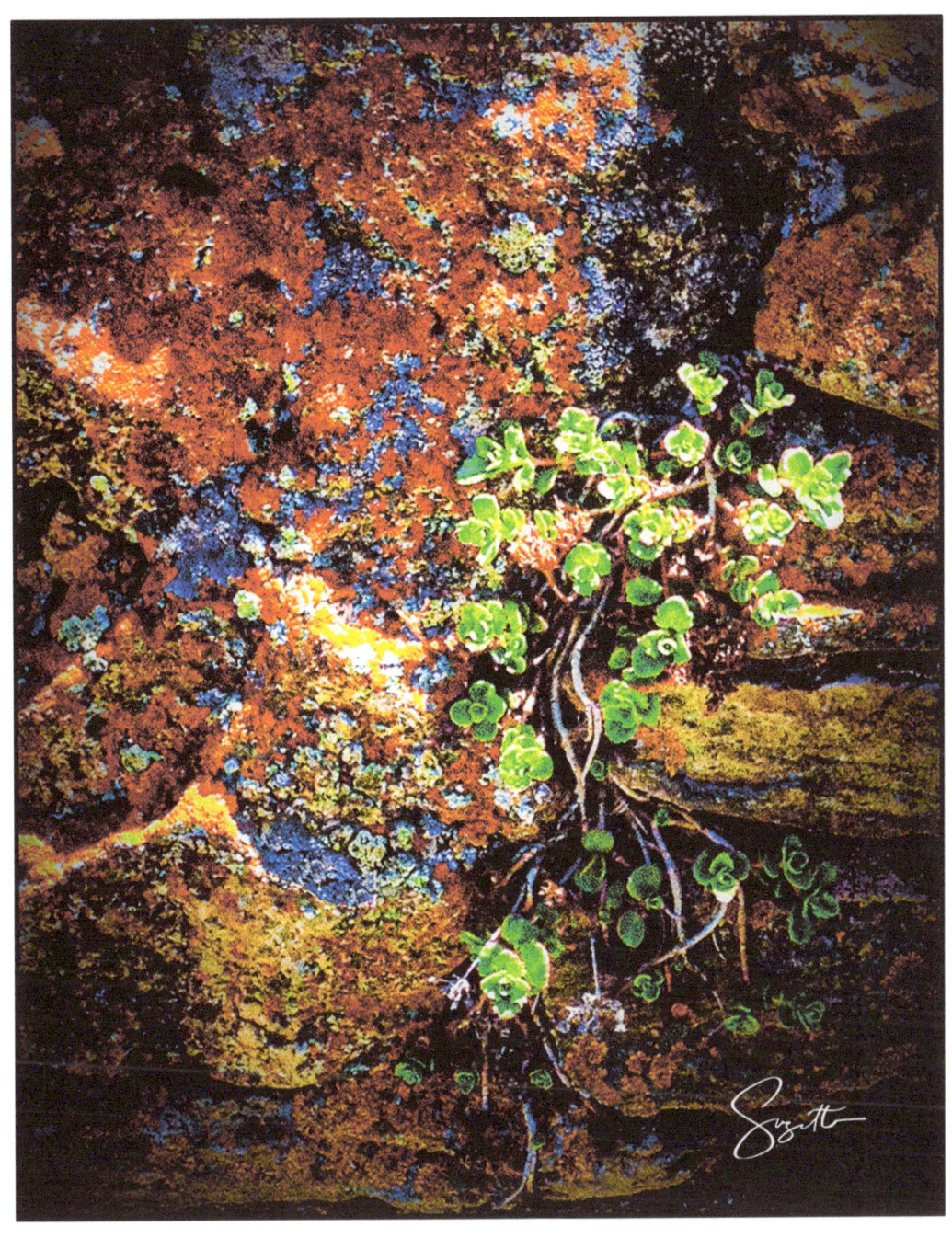

"I can describe a better world by better seeing the world in front of me."
~Robert Adams.

During the shutdown, I practiced yoga on YouTube in a makeshift studio at home.
In one of the sessions, the instructor said something to the extent of,
'losing balance to advance in our practice.'

I lose my balance a lot, both in yoga and in life.
But as I toppled over in 'Warrior 3' that day, it seemed ok.
It occurred to me that I wouldn't know balance without UNbalance.

It's all ok.
Losing our balance with everything we've come to know,
and then finding ourselves stronger on the other side.

It's ok to topple. That's how we grow.

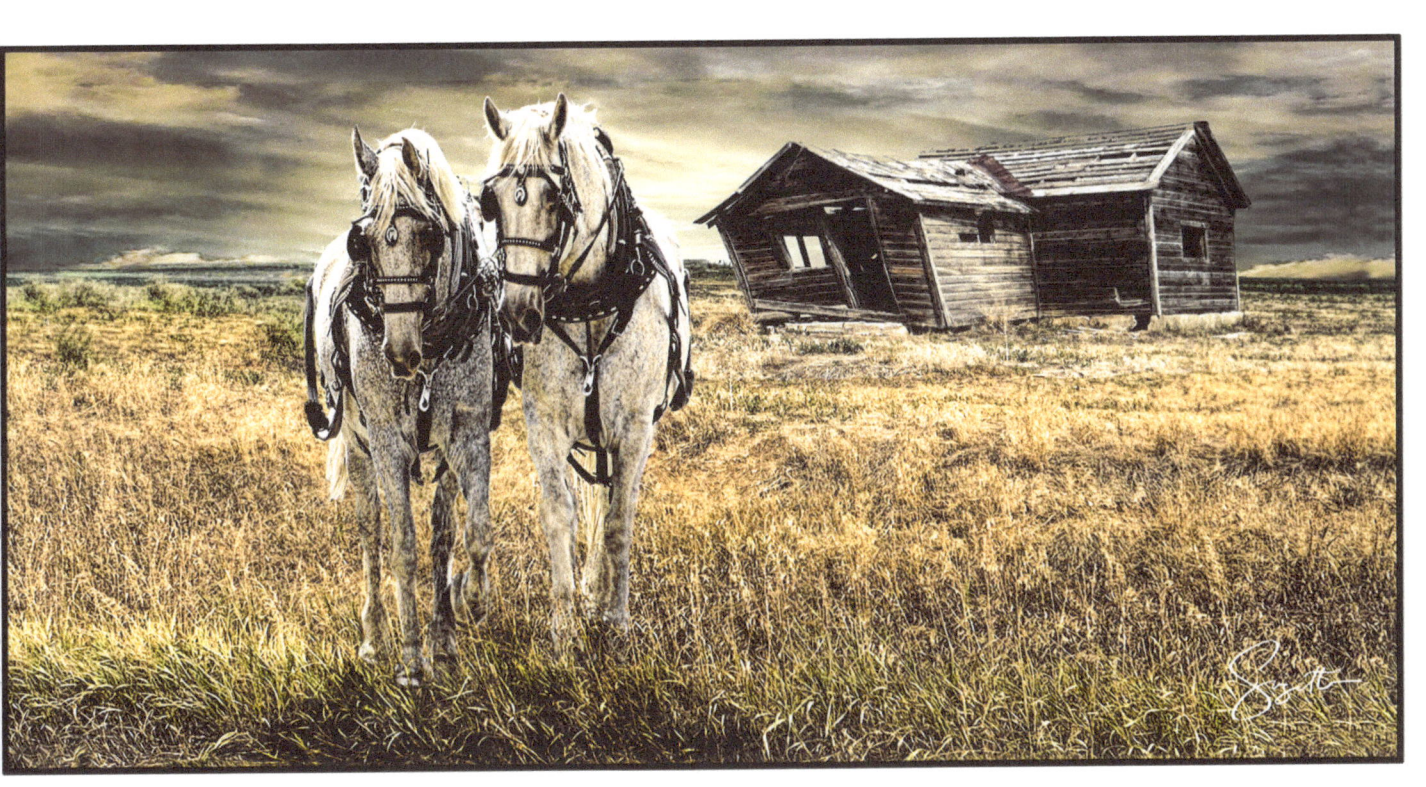

"I needed to lose my balance to find it."
~ Suzette

Struggle and fear are more about the unknown than anything else; the inability to see what lies ahead.

During the pandemic of 2020, I struggled with unknowns: What does isolation mean? How long will this last? How much food should I store up? Will we ever come out of this? Will I get the virus? Will I die from it? What if someone I know dies from it... I'm afraid.

There were opportunities in this struggle. Although it was difficult on so many levels,
the isolation was freeing. There was no place I needed to be. It was a time that I was able to slow down from all the chaos and recharge.

The pandemic began slow and spread so quickly that it cracked the world into pieces. God used the opportunity to wedge between the cracks, infiltrate, widen the space, loosen up the pace, and create TIME.

Time had disappeared, and Time is what God is.

The world slowed down for a bit and reinvented itself from its entanglement. Isolation was restoration.

Embrace the space of struggle,
knowing there's so much more on the other side.

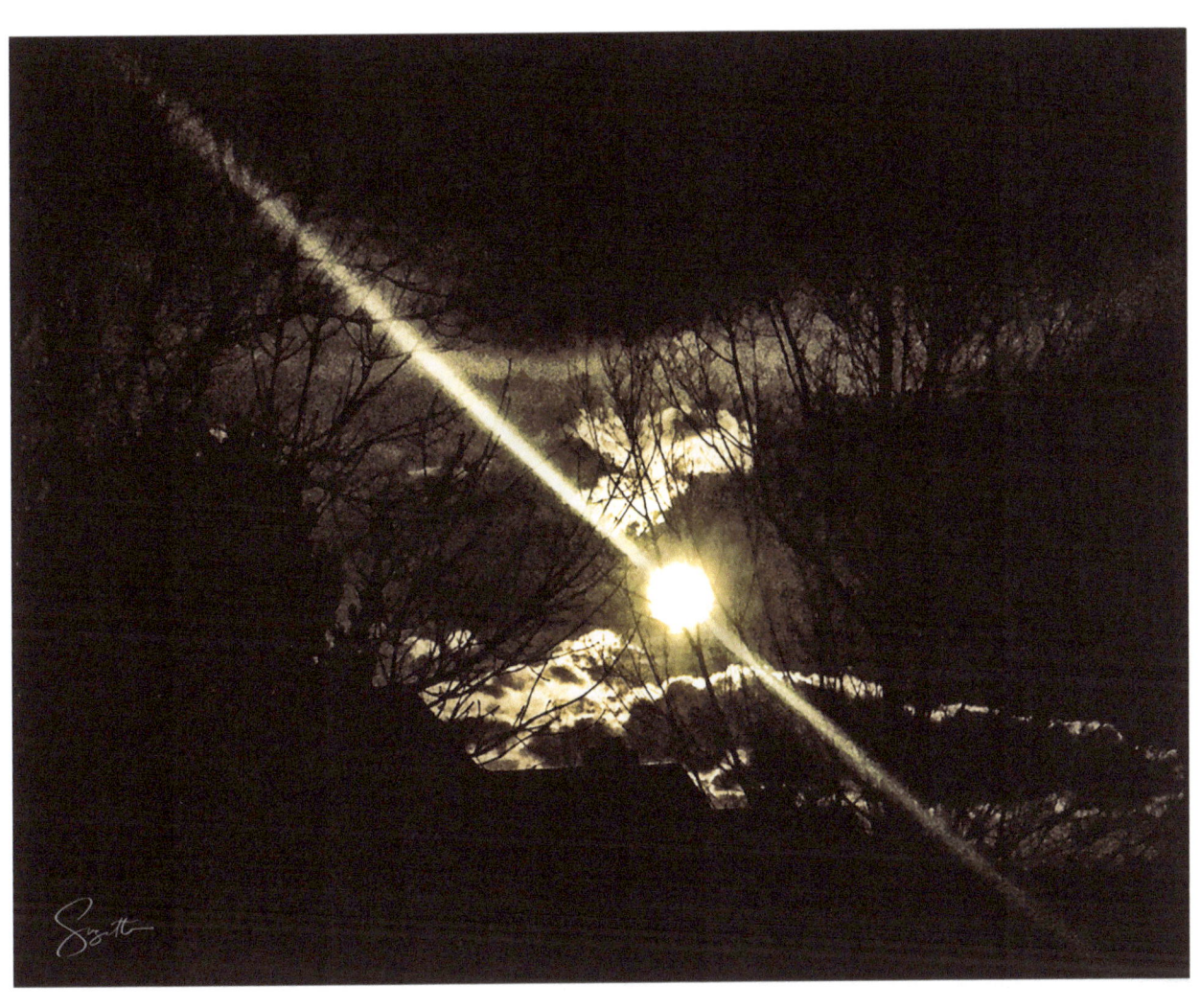

"Opportunity follows struggle."
~ Shelby Steele

It was a complete white-out as I drove through a snowstorm
in Steamboat Springs, Colorado.

I was on my way to snowshoe, and my mind was busy on the day ahead,
not noticing much of anything else.

I glanced through my thoughts into the outside blizzard
and saw this incredible scene.

It nipped me back to reality and the beauty I had missed
by blurring out the present moment.

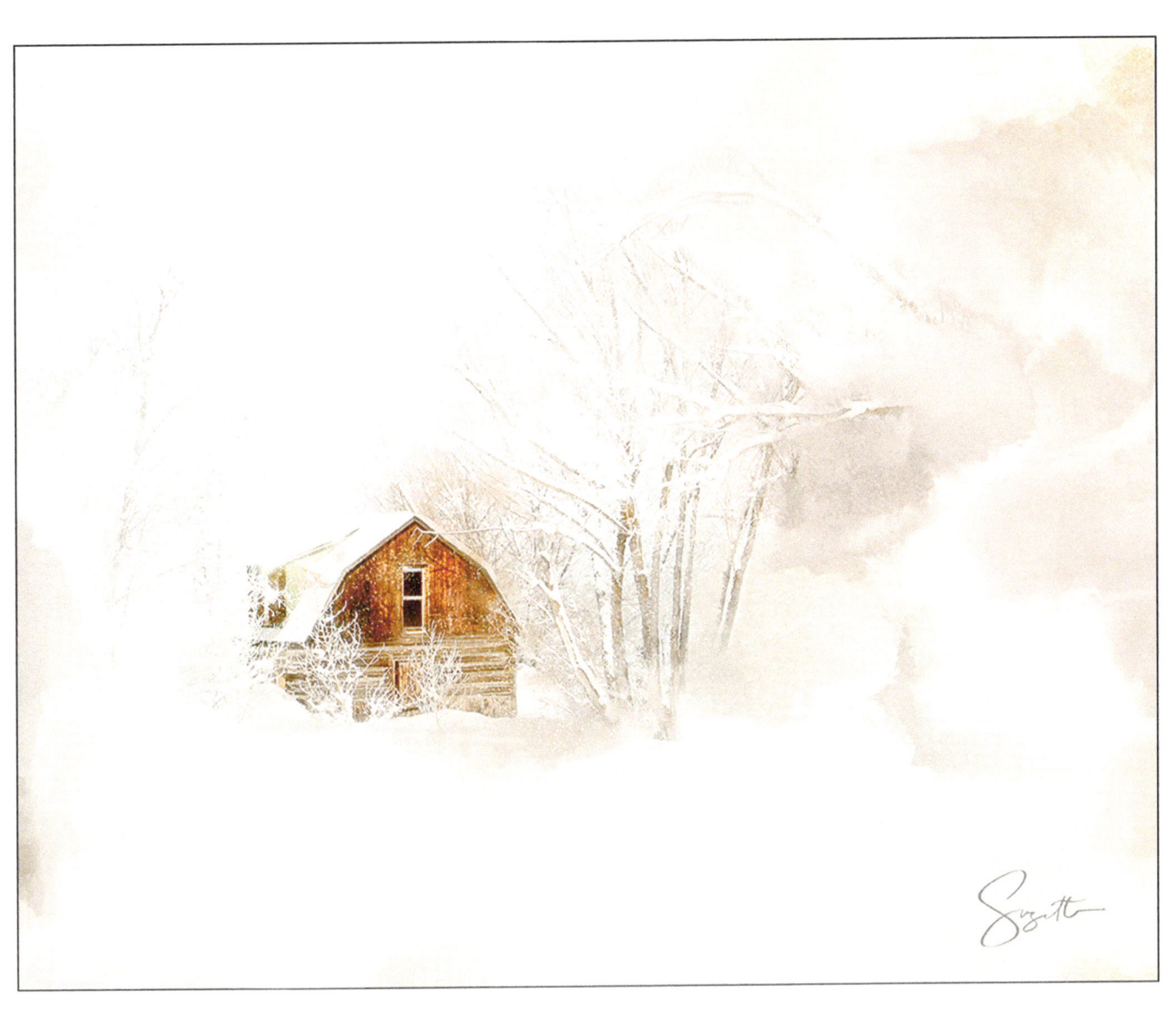

"Always be on the lookout for the presence of wonder."
~E.B.White

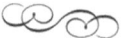

Our capacity to love is never-ending.
There is always something more.
Look beyond,
and you will see beauty wrapped in every situation.

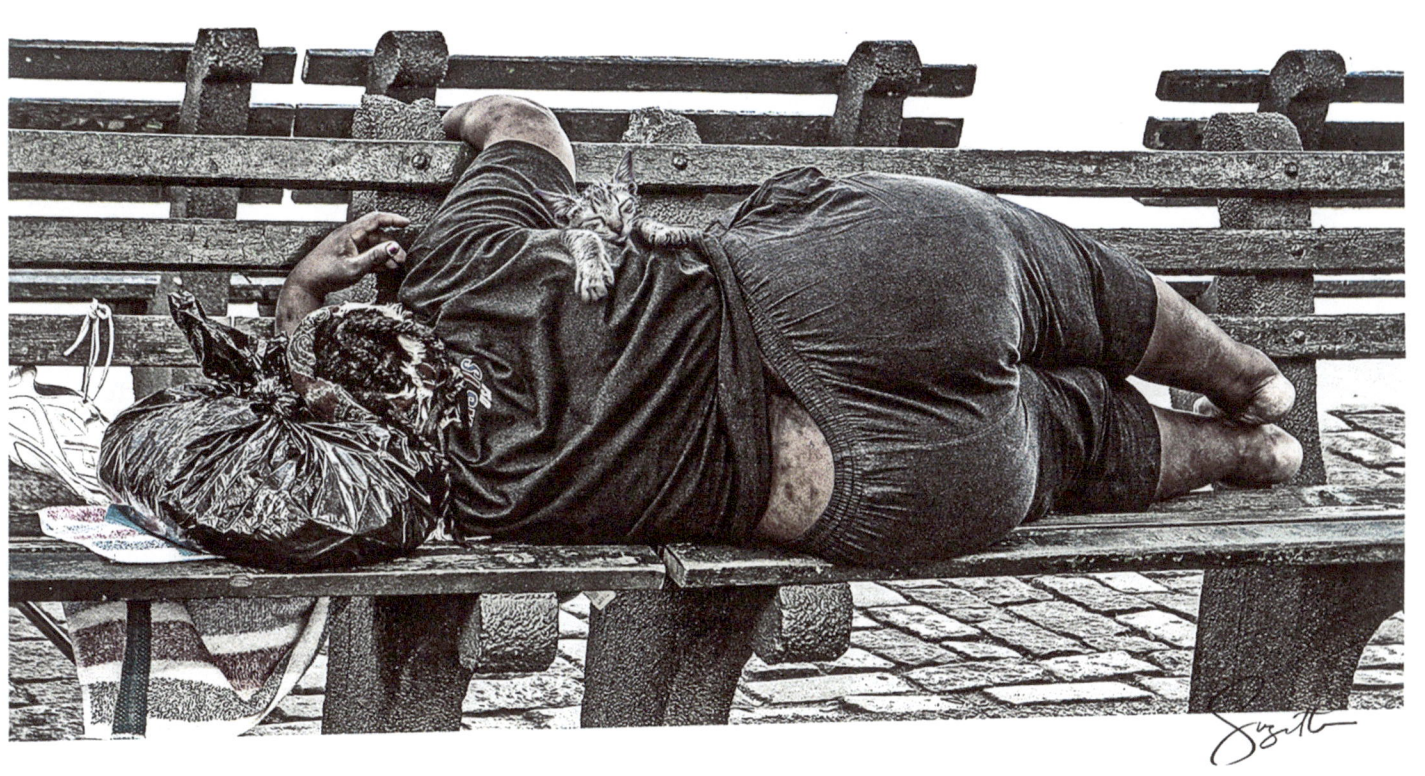

"Where there is love there is life."
~Mahatma Gandhi

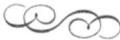

Vision goes far beyond sight.
We see what lies before us, but the mind takes over and judges.
Judgment creates blindness to what is.
Our mind will not allow the full circumference of vision.

We have merely touched the outer periphery of our abilities
until we learn to look beyond the obvious,
seeing with more than just our eyes.

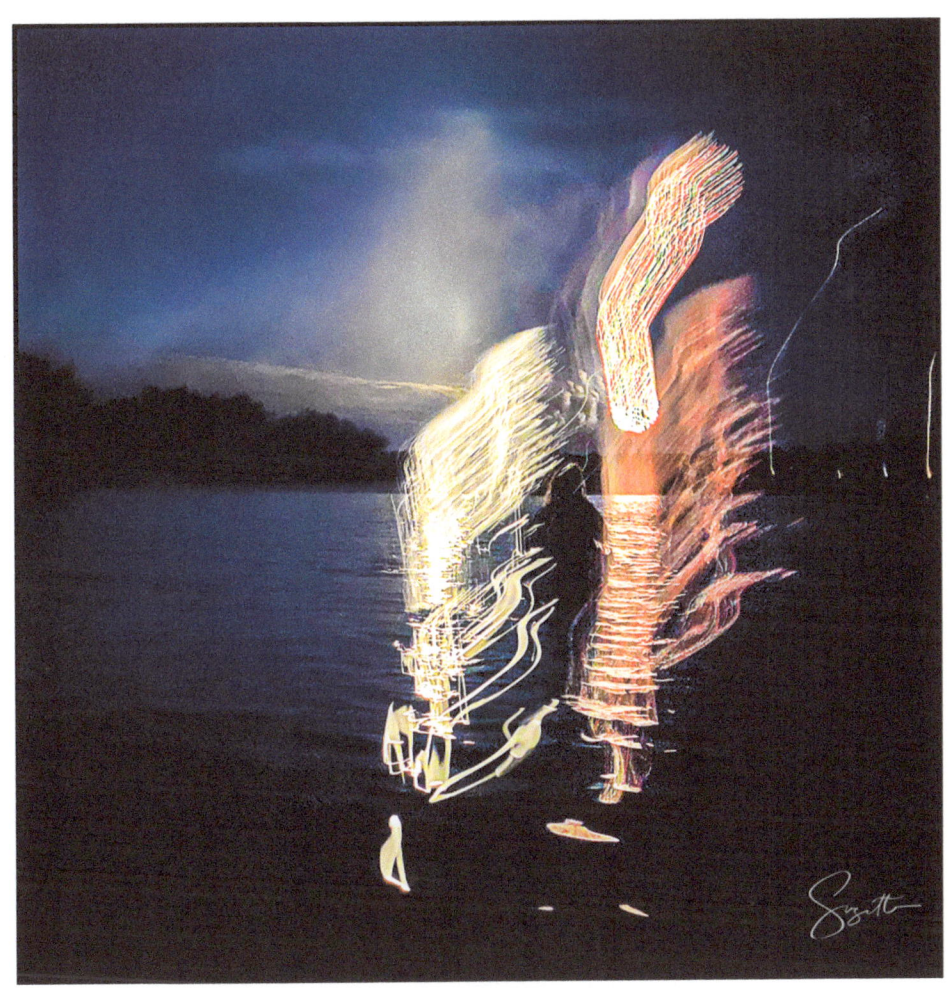

"*Vision is the art of seeing the invisible.*"
~ Jonathan Swift

There is no right or wrong. It just is.
Letting go of the feeling that we should have an opinion about every little thing opens us up to the ability to experience the pleasure of contentment.

When I catch myself in the miserable state of judgementalism,
I try to remind myself that it's not my deal.

Funny enough, that one simple thought unleashes me to move beyond,
into the carefree field of acceptance.

I'll meet you there.

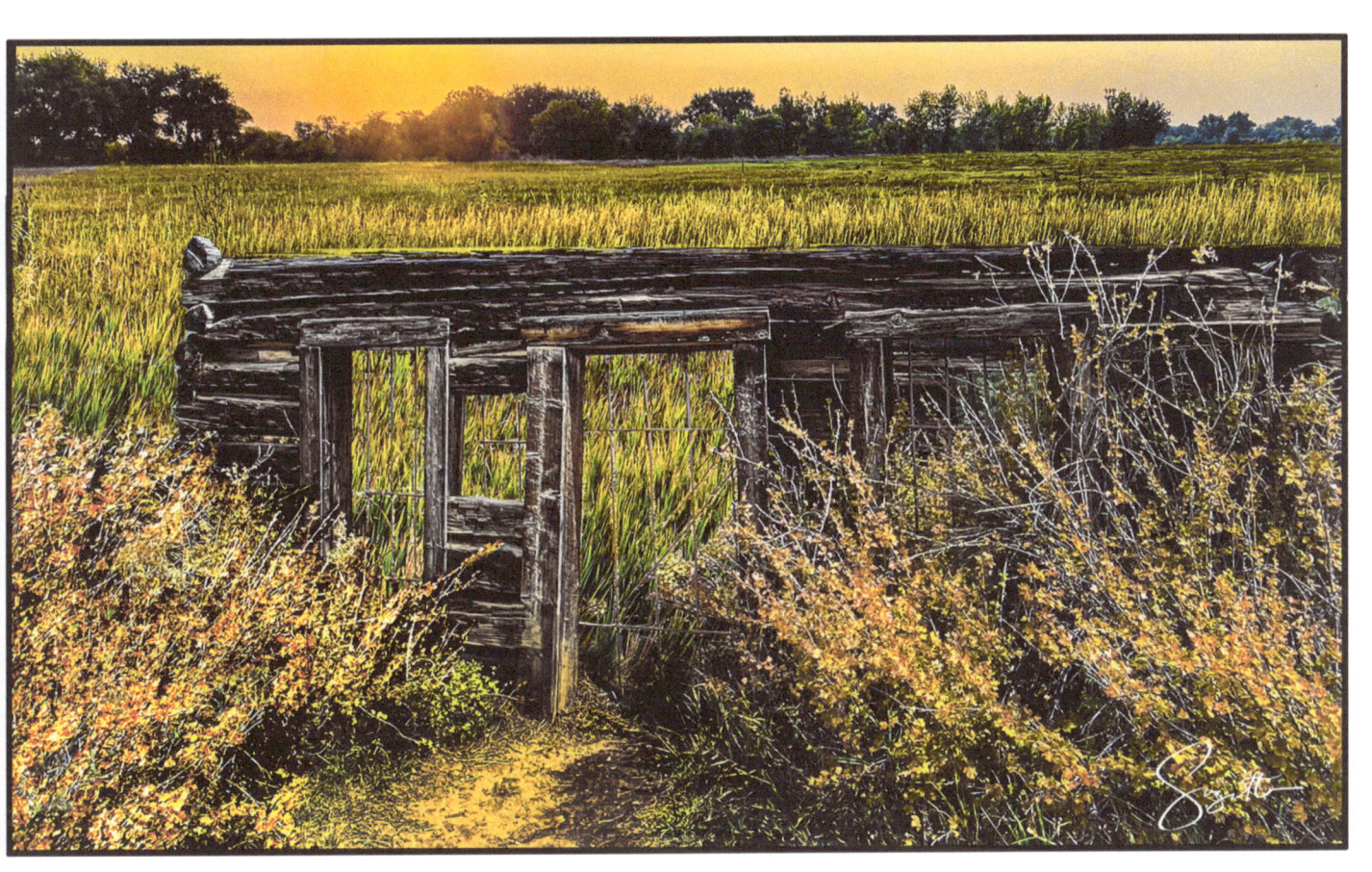

"Out beyond ideas of wrongdoing and rightdoing there is a field.
...I'll meet you there."
~Rumi

I love this mug. It's one of my favorites.
When I use it, I contemplate what it says,
remembering how many 'PLAN B's' I've had to utilize in my lifetime,
where nothing goes as planned.

I have a choice in how to handle these disruptions.
I can bury myself in misery, or I can swerve and start again.

The choices weave the tapestry of my life.

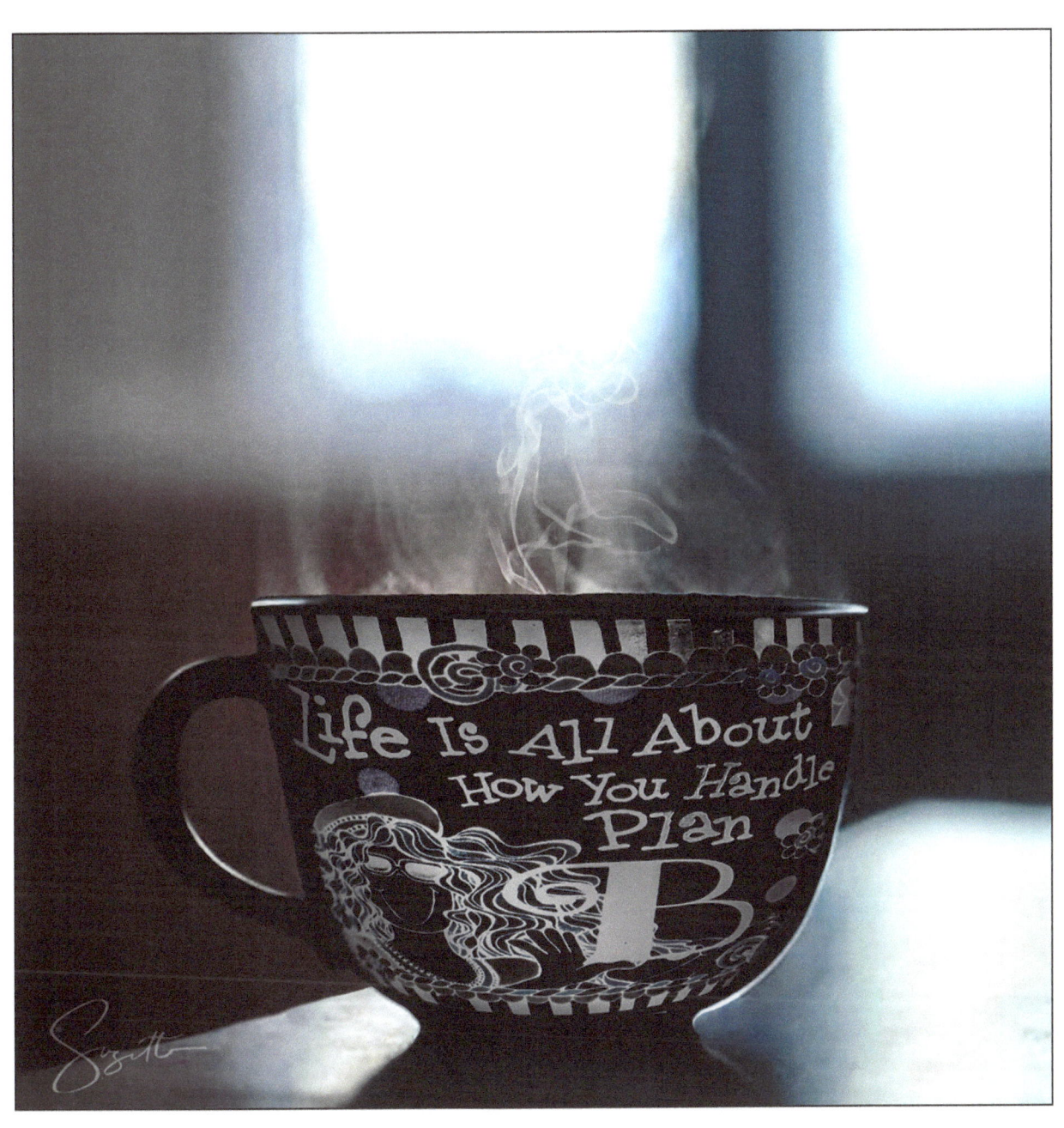

"Life is all about how you handle plan B."
~ Suzy Toronto

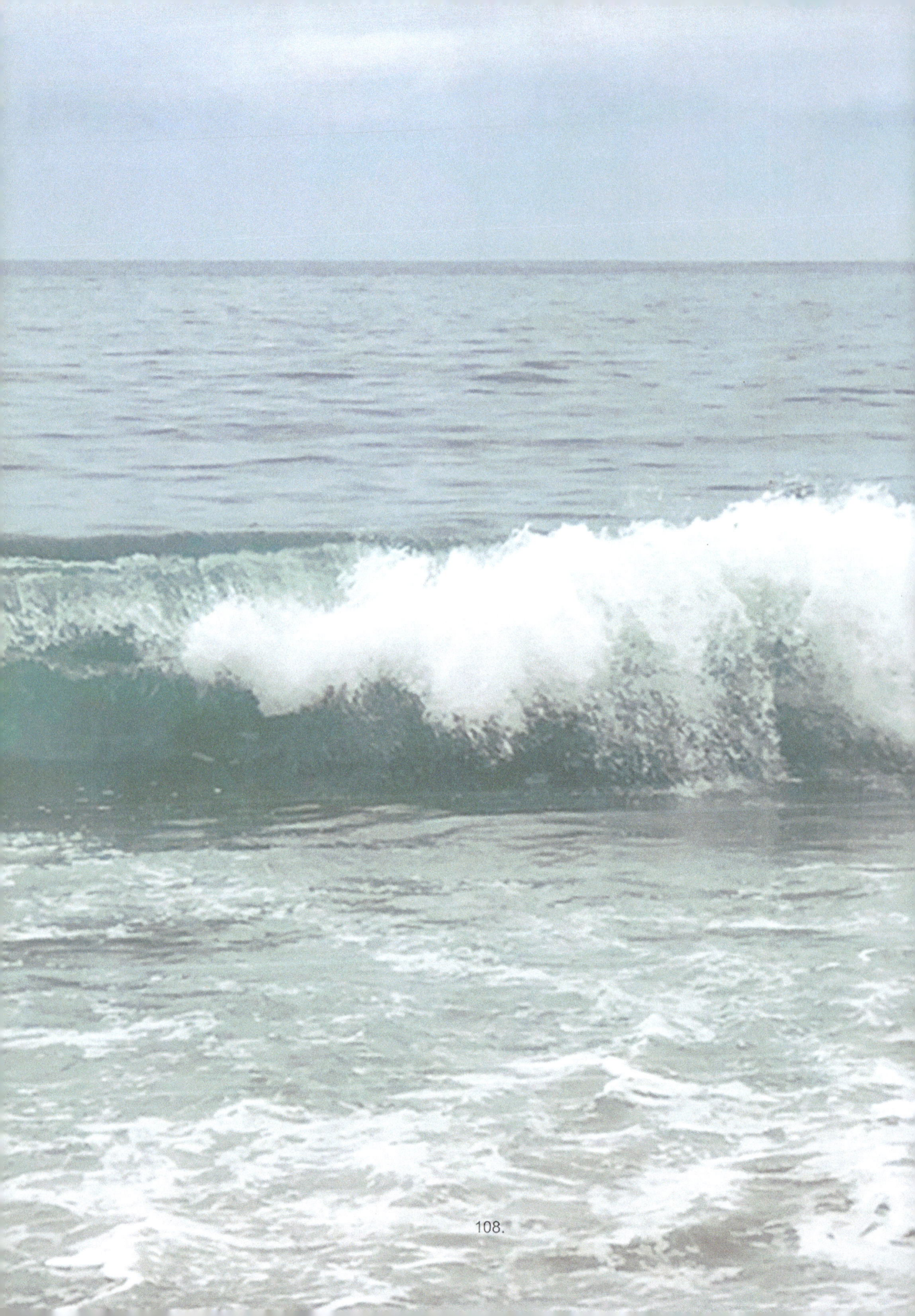

Water

You've stepped beyond the chaos, and moving inward, what do you hear?

We can learn from listening to the sea. It contains magic. This magic makes water soft enough to caress you yet powerful enough to wear away stone.

This magic immerses itself in a quiet lake to bring you stillness, and throws itself into the movement of a river to inspire the flow of thought.

This magic also hovers in an ocean's vastness to expand perception and remind you that you're part of something greater than yourself.

Use the magic of water to listen.

The art of being alive is knowing when to go deep and when to dance with the waves.

"Dance with the waves, move with the sea.
Let the rhythm of the water set your soul free."
~Christy Ann Martine

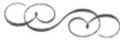

By moving inward and listening to the flow within,
you can rise above the noise
and merge with the wholeness of the present moment
where all answers lie.

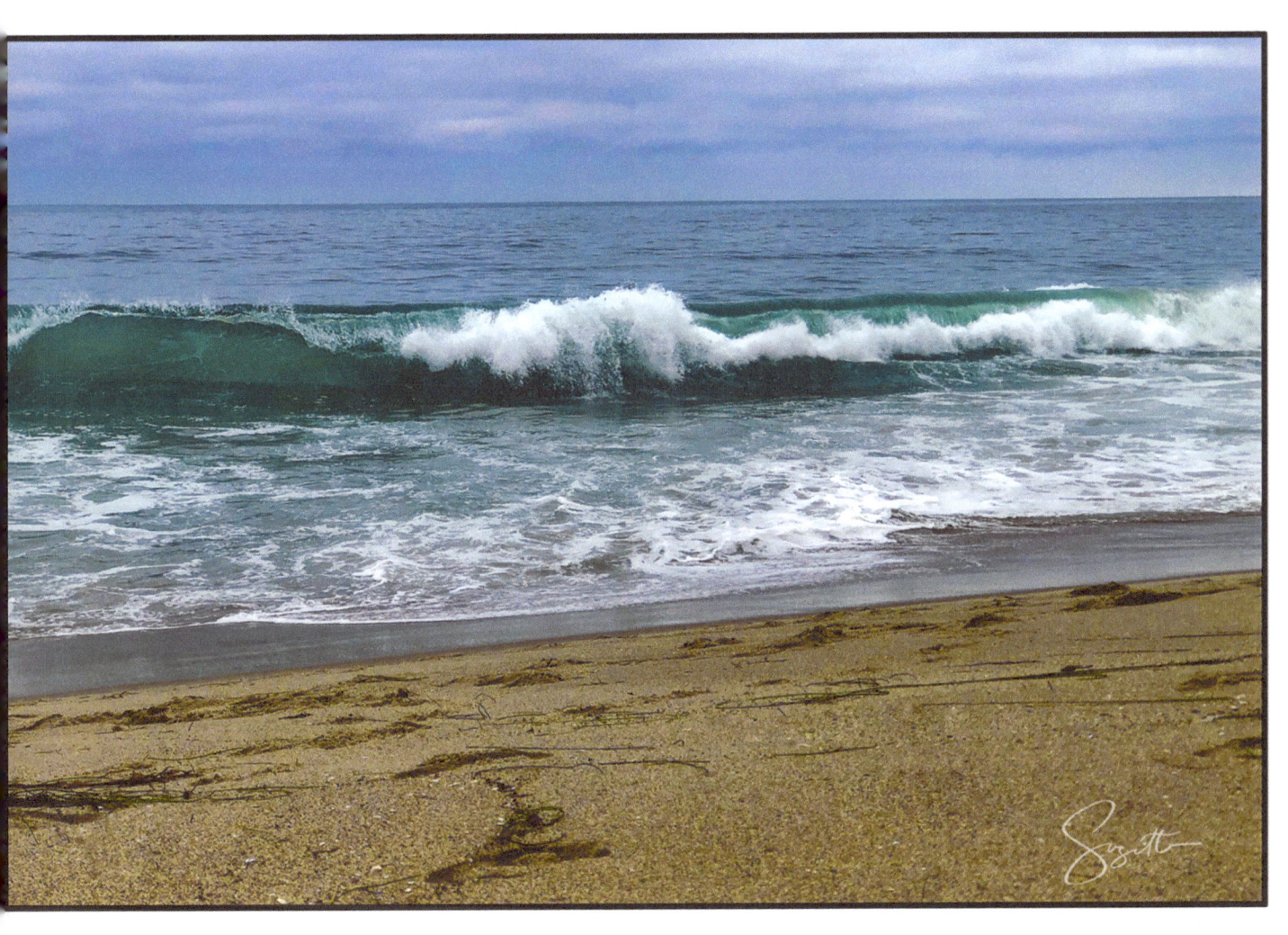

"Listen to the sound of waves within you."
~Rumi

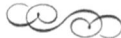

Looking down deep inside yourself,
you will find the mastery and solitude of a Universal Power.

There are answers. There are words. There is direction.

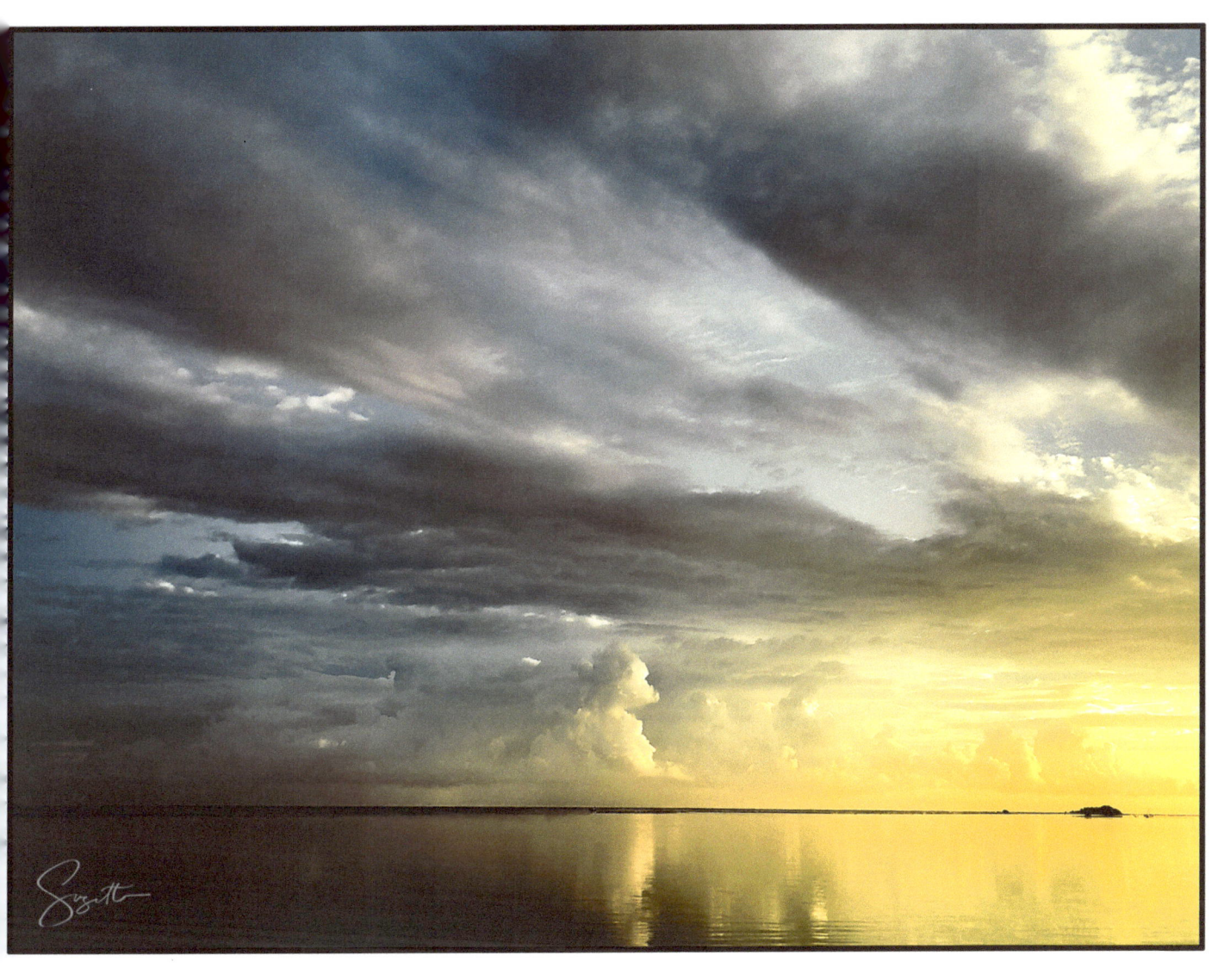

"We are like islands in the sea, separate on the surface but connected in the deep."
~ William James

Knowing there's a Universal Force within us is empowering.
There's no need to struggle for power or approval.

You are complete.
You can simply 'be', moving about the day with peace and confidence.

Staying focused on this Inner Power will create a peaceful, powerful aura –
a disposition that cannot be affected or penetrated by any force.

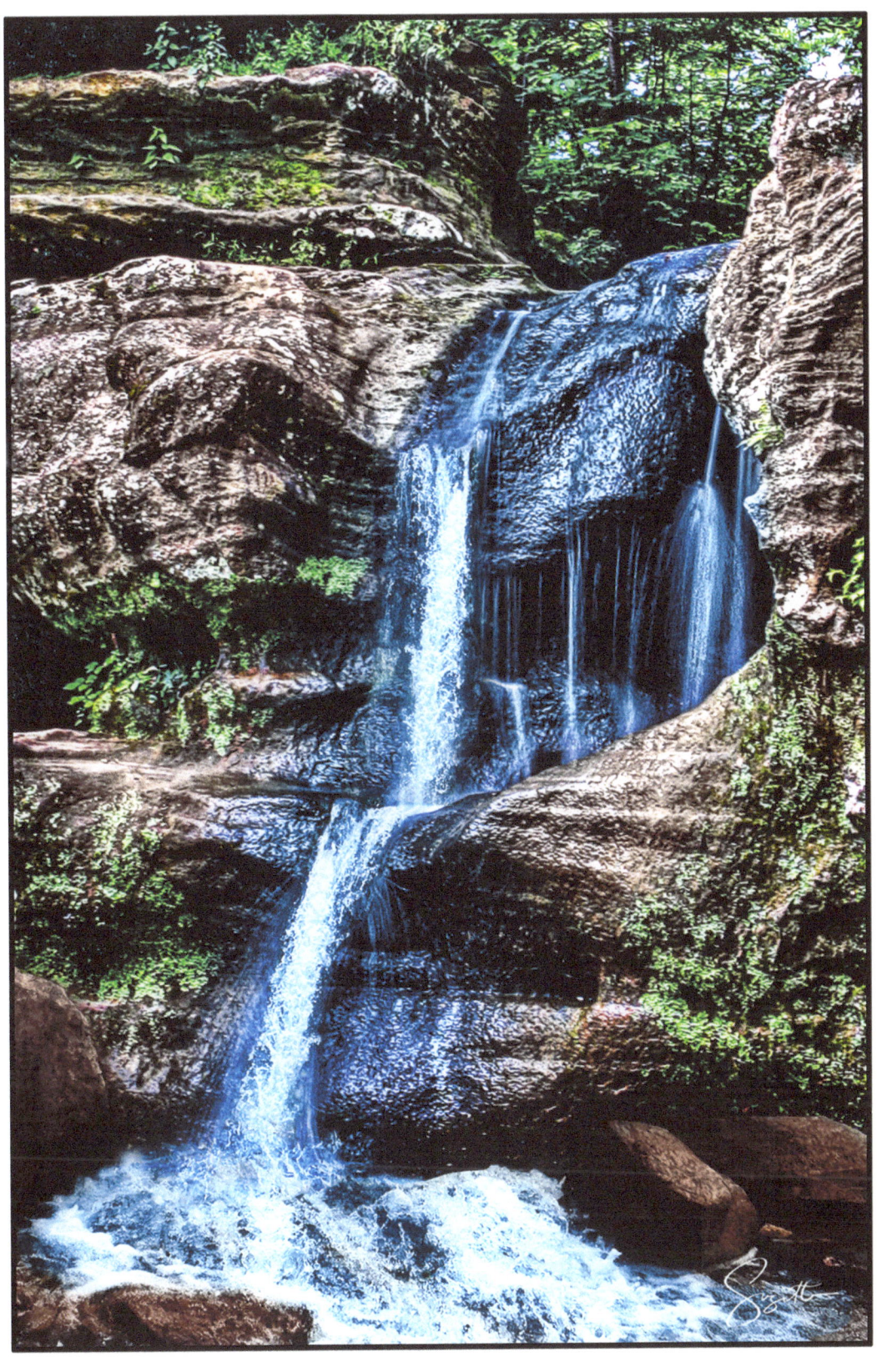

"The softest things in the world overcome the hardest things in the world."
~ Lao Tzu

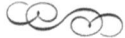

If you're steadfast and unaffected,
no one can diminish your peaceful state of mind.

If you're ok, everything surrounding you will also be ok.

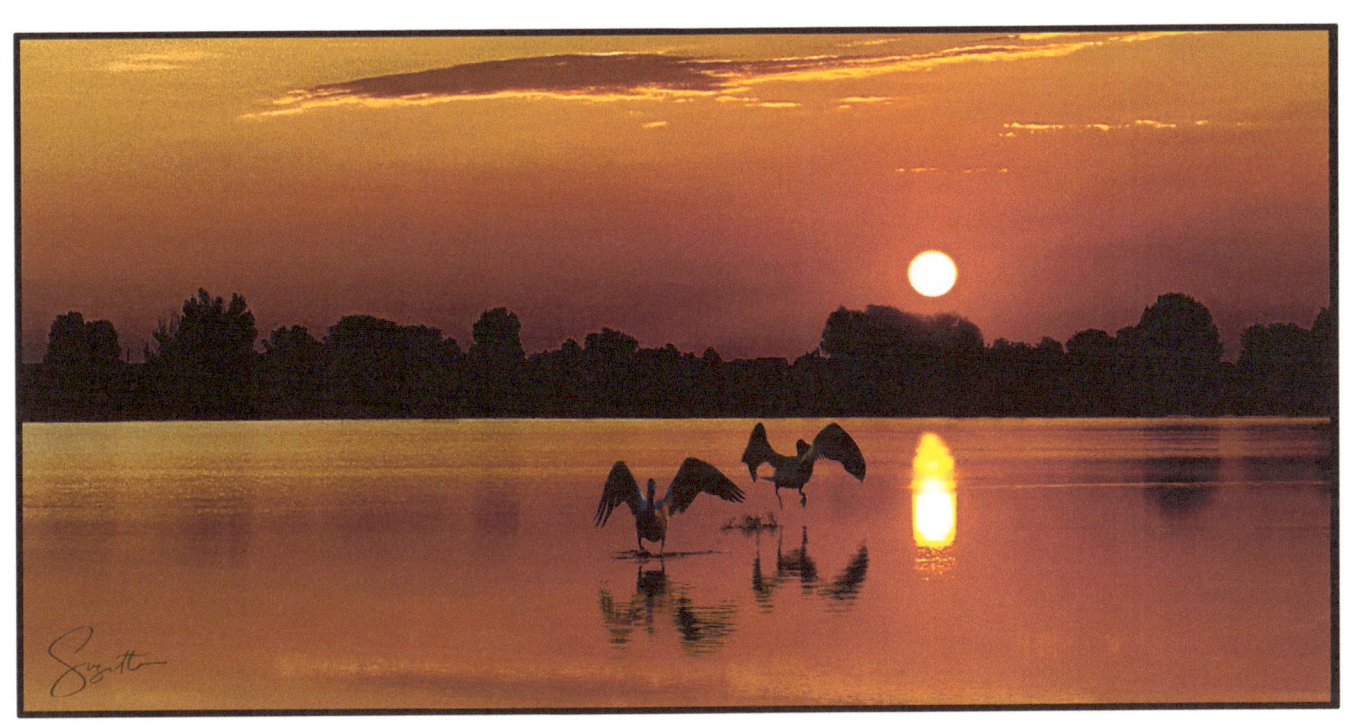

"No one can see their reflection in running water. It is only in still water that we can see."
~ Taoist proverb

Don't be afraid to love, to put yourself out there.
Bring it up from the depths of your Source.
Go out there and do what you need to do with unselfish kindness and compassion.
The knowledge of this Power from within is enough to keep you elevated.
Response and recognition will no longer be necessary.

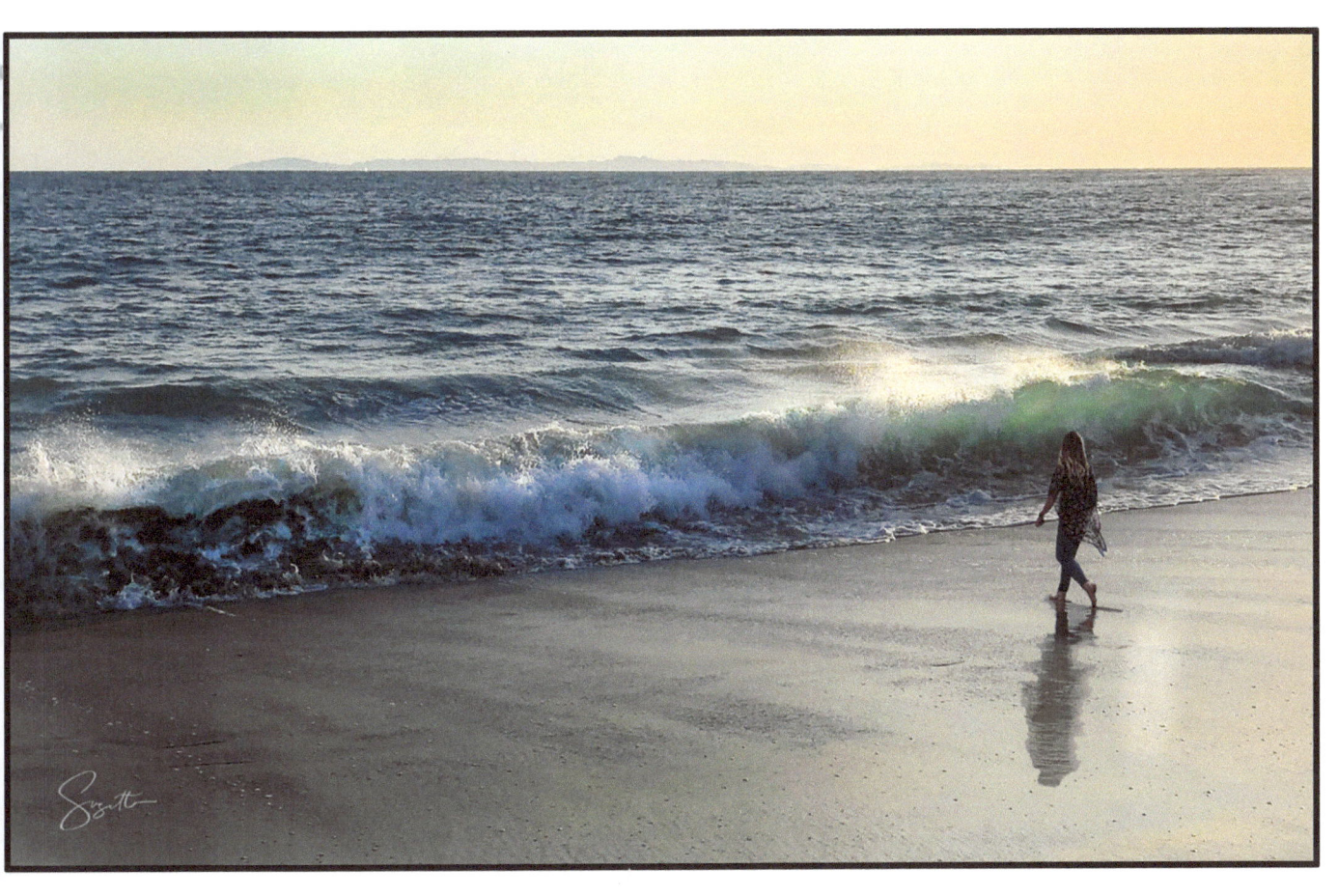

*We are not being manipulated by outside powerful forces:
We ourselves are the powerful force."
~Leo Buscaglia*

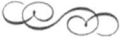

Fragility creates surrender.
It wears down our rough edges
into a deeper level of compassion and patience.

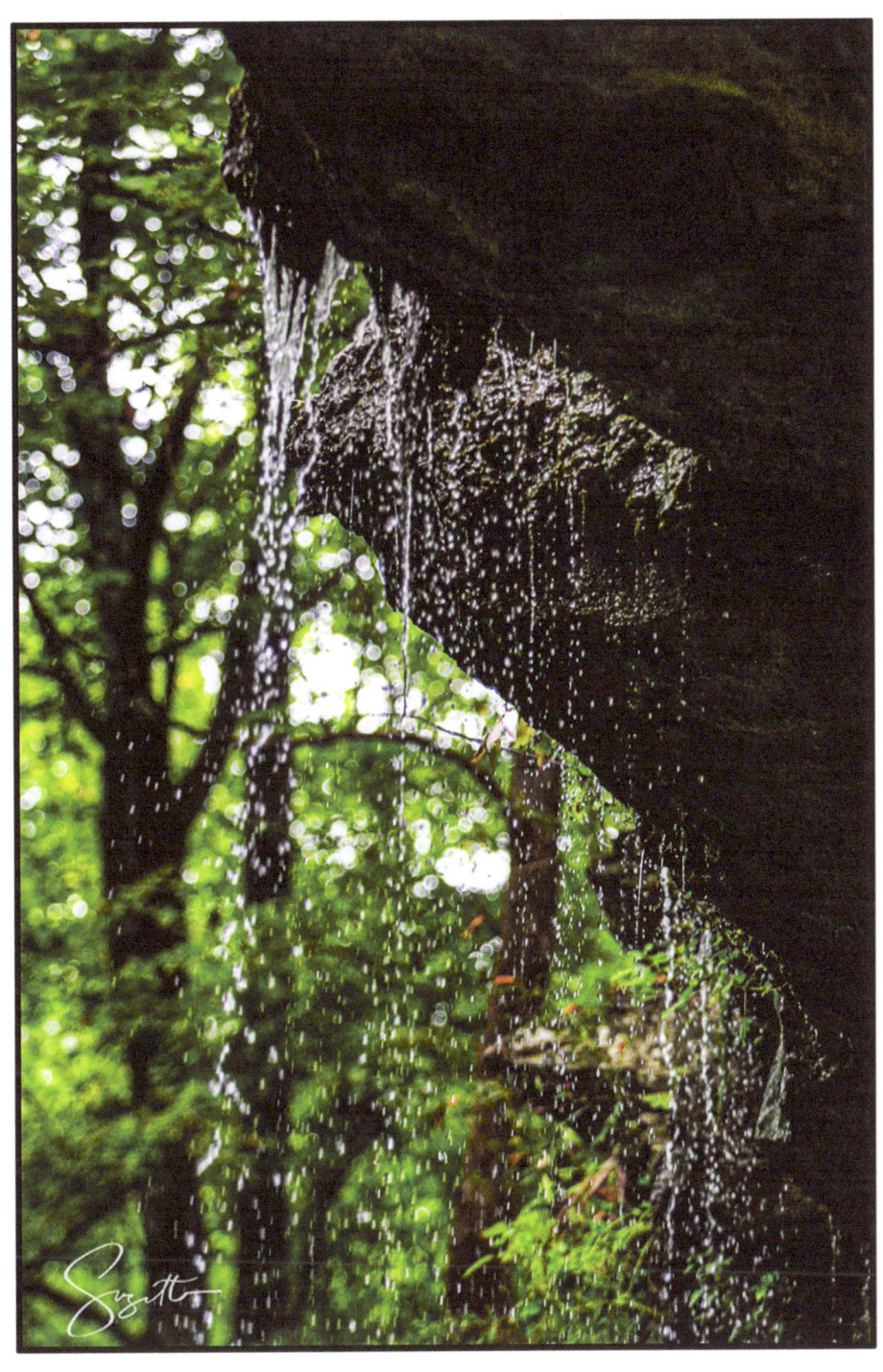

"Do not feel sad for your tears as rocks never regret the waterfalls."
~ Munia Khan

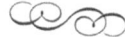

When you're here experiencing this moment
there is no need to be anywhere else.

This moment is whole.
This moment is complete.
Wrap yourself up in it and then let it go.

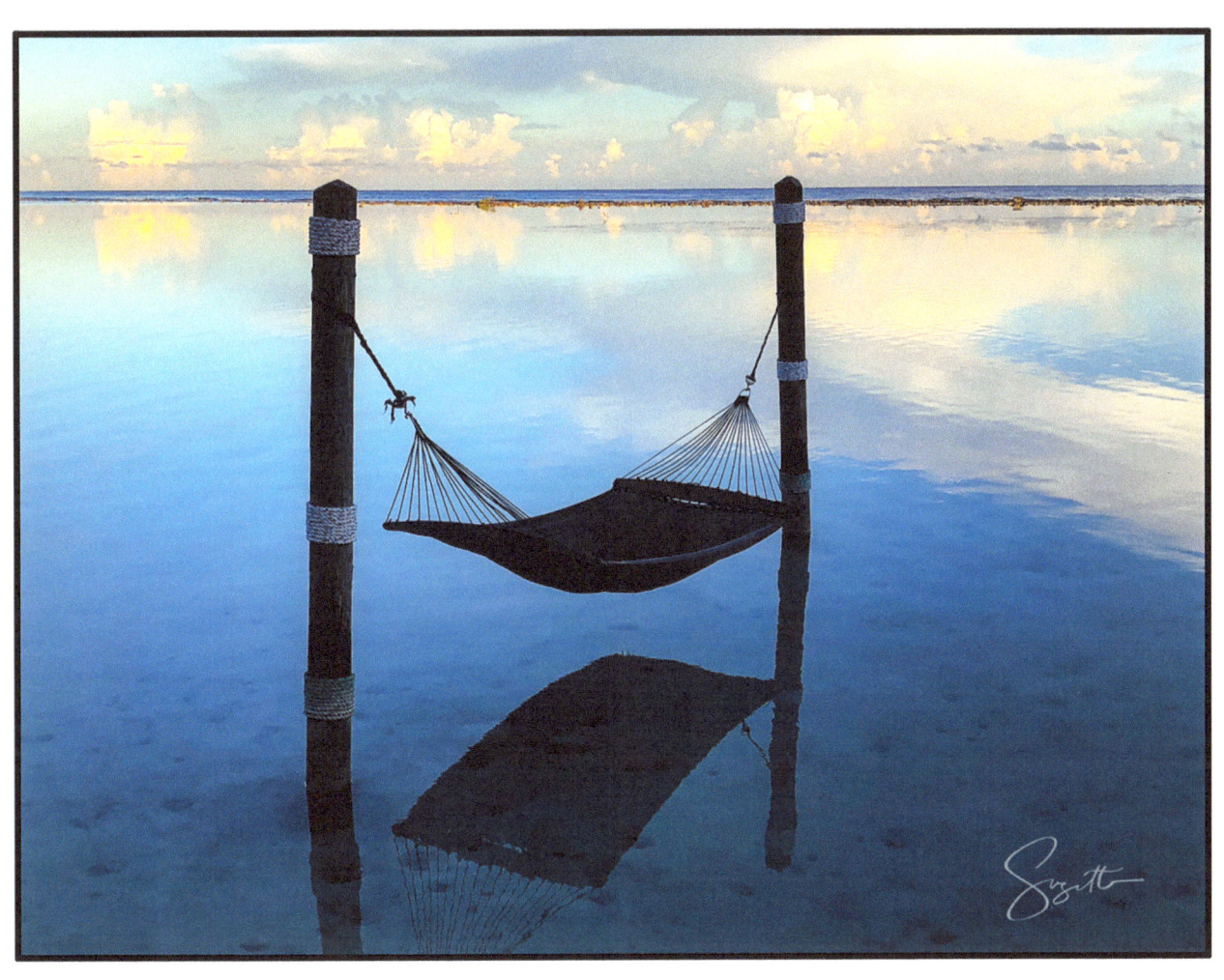

"Realize deeply that the present moment is all you will ever have."
~Eckhart Tolle

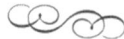

The mind is like water.
When it's disconnected from the flow within,
it races into discomfort and goes where it wants to go.
The mind can destroy anything in its path when its
allowed to run rampant.

This disconnect is easy because it takes no work.
We simply tap into the external and allow it to
dictate the day.

With this permissive disposition, emotions acquiesce to
whatever forces come into our physical and conscience
plane.

Peace comes from tapping into the inward flow, not outward circumstances.

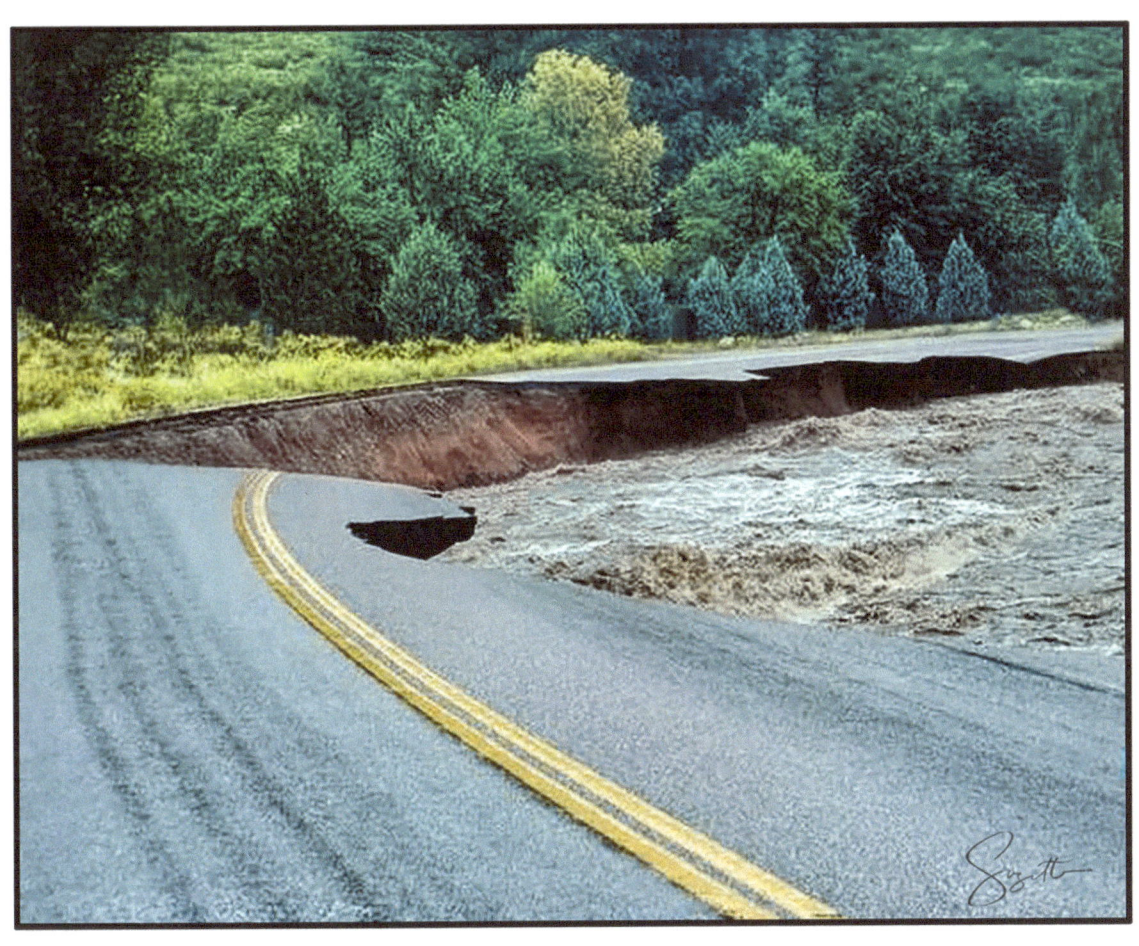

*"Water always goes where it wants to go,
and nothing in the end can stand against it."
~Margaret Atwood*

We hear that we're supposed to slow down and 'go with the flow', but with life moving at such a fast pace, do you fear you'll be left in the dust if you slow down too much?

Imagine placing yourself into the simplicity of the natural flow, the whole.

When you become part of the whole, there is no separation. There's only awareness in this present moment.

If you submit to the fast pace, there's clamor. There's confusion. You'll miss opportunities in the chaos of the day.

If you stand in this moment, there's calm. There's clarity. Circumstances and people will be placed before you.

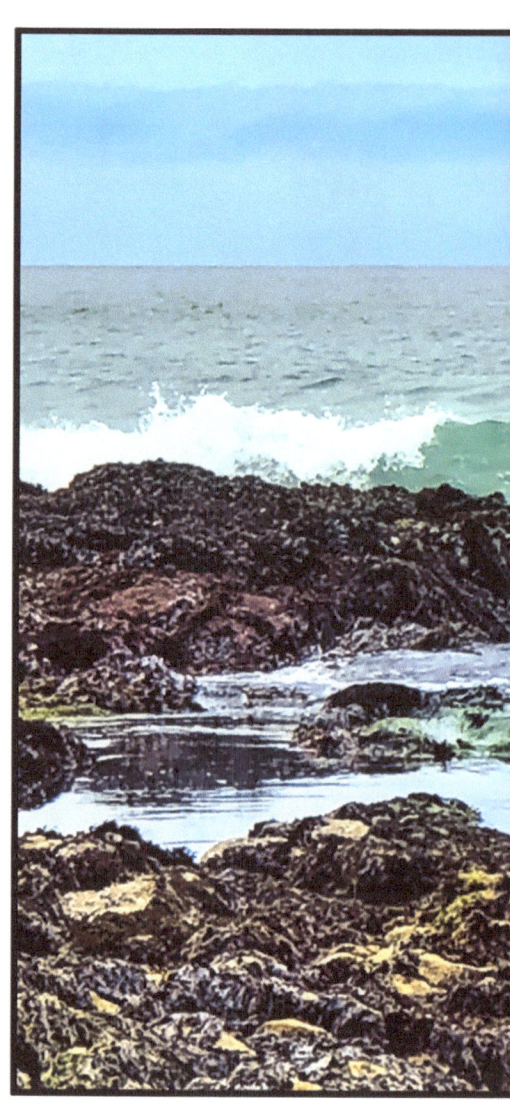

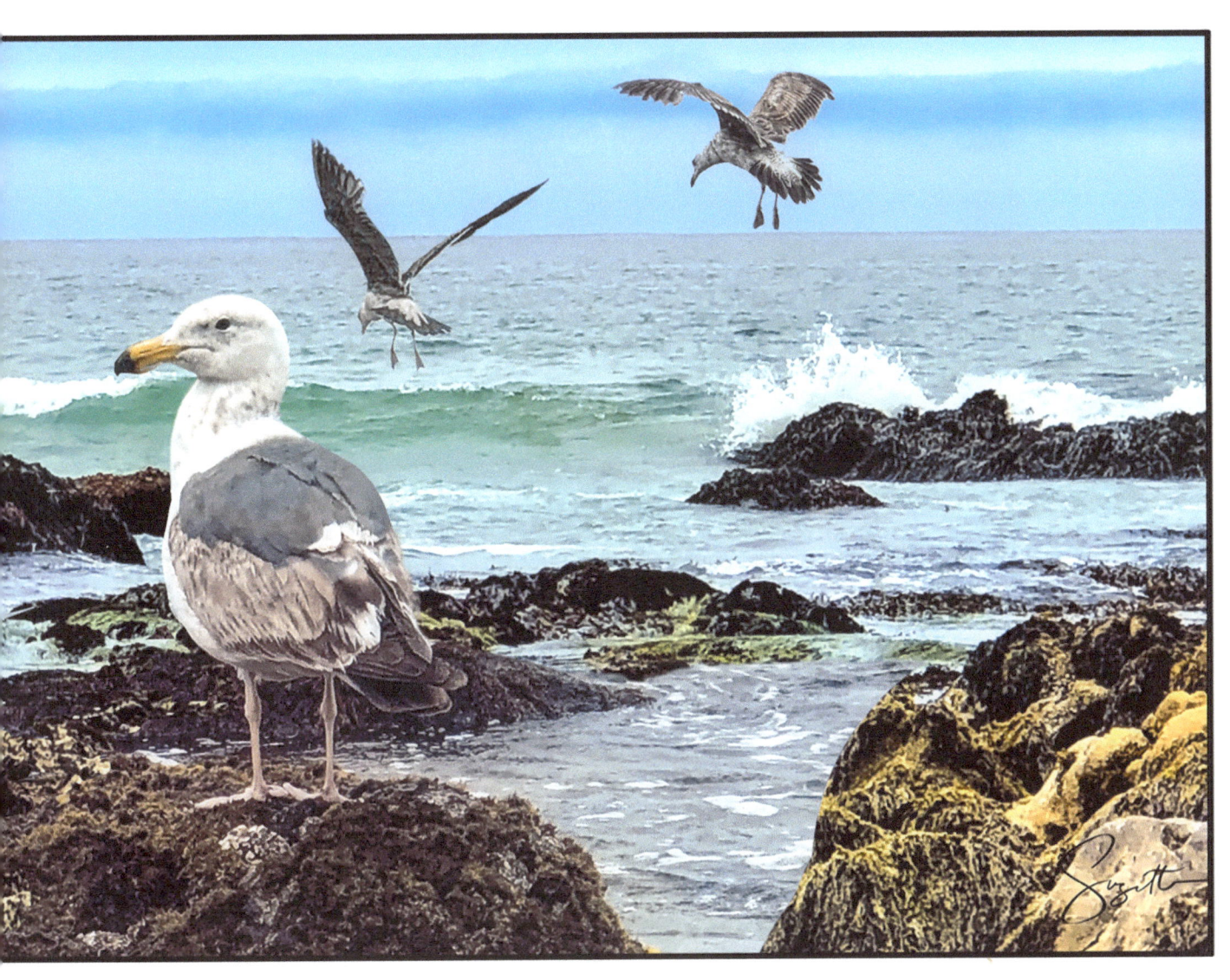

"If you don't become the ocean, you'll be seasick everyday."
~Leonard Cohen

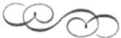

Nothing is impossible.
With the darkness of the world outside you,
your infinite supply of energy comes from within.

You will never leave you.
Your Source is endless.

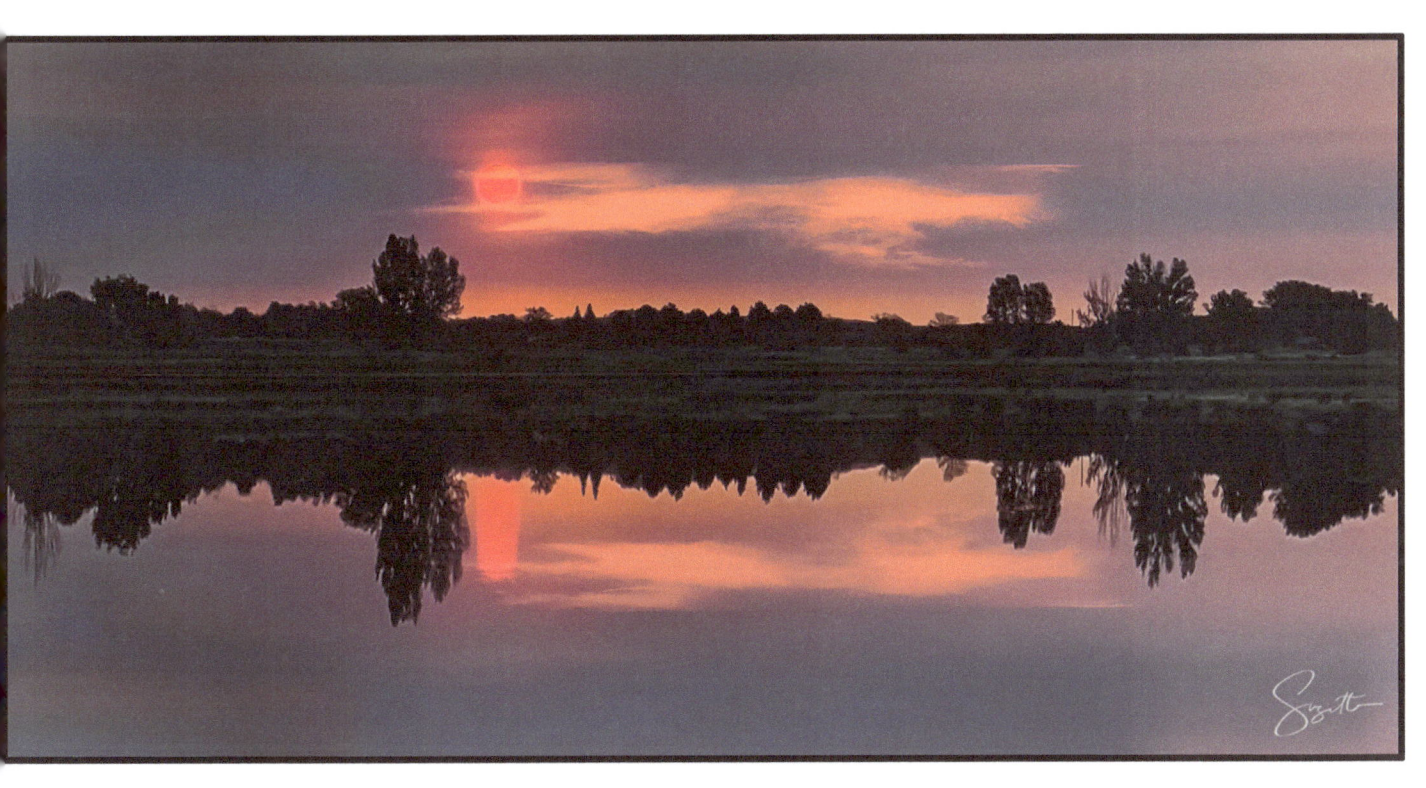

"Only from your heart can you touch the sky."
~Rumi

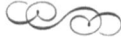

A constant dialog with your soul; the Infinite Power within, will diminish your walls so that your light can shine through and become more visible to the people you come in contact with throughout the day.

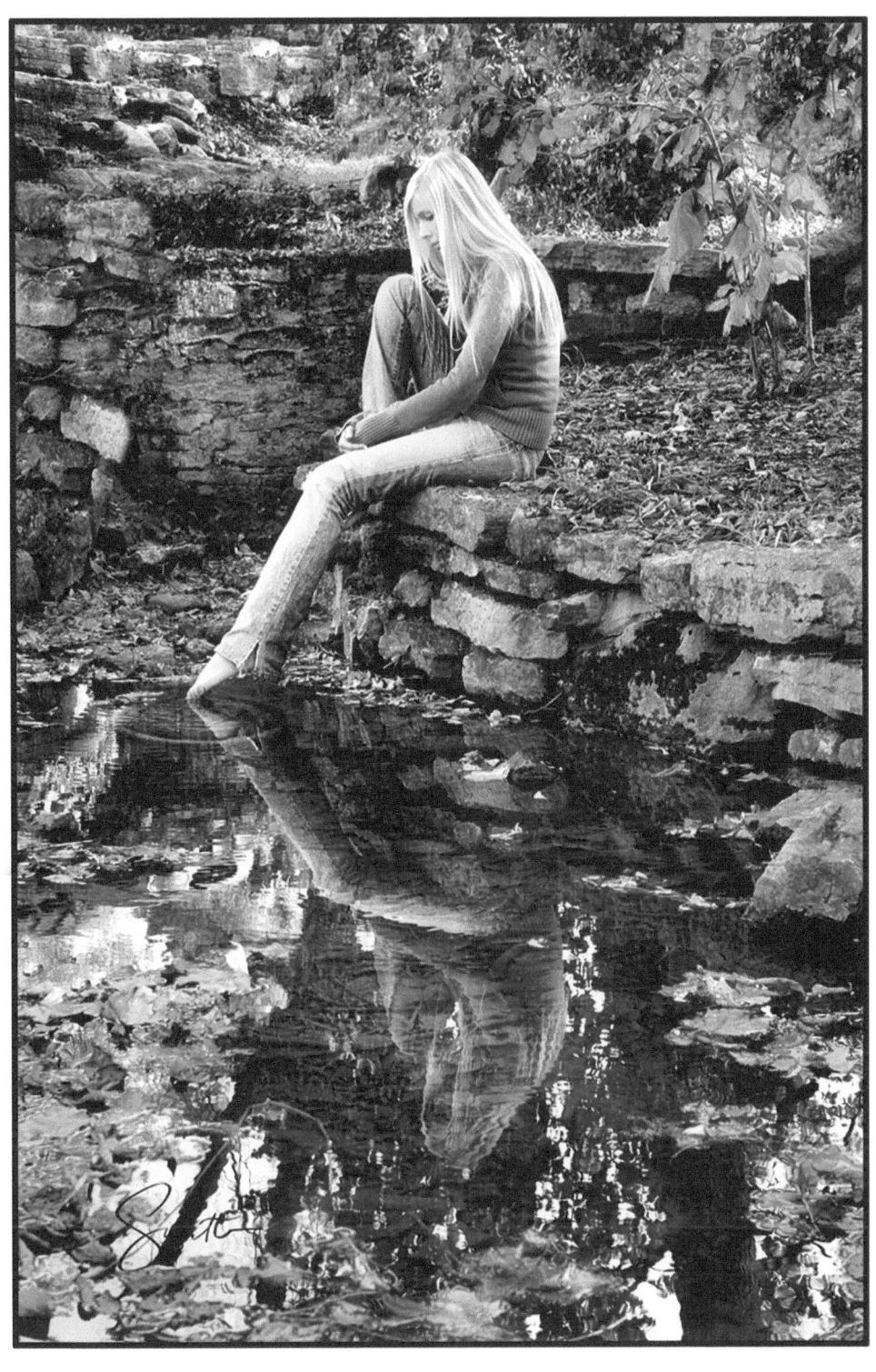

'As water reflects the face, so one's life reflects the heart'.
Proverbs 27:19

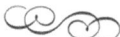

With issues coming from all directions,
daily circumstances can still bring us down.
But if you continue to focus on why you're here,
you'll encounter Power greater than yourself.

Rise above the insignificant earthly affairs.
Realize what you can do nothing about in this life
and let it go.

Move forward and boldly keep your eyes on your purpose.

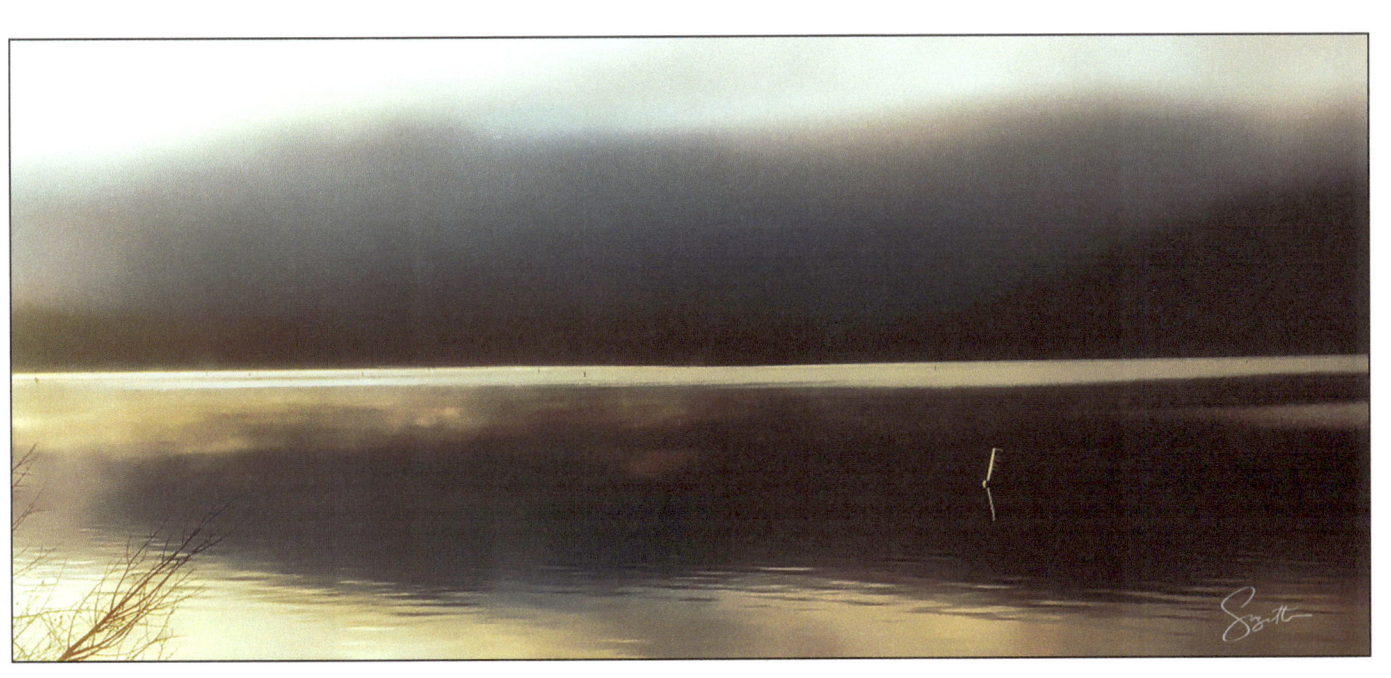

"Courage is knowing what not to fear."
~Plato

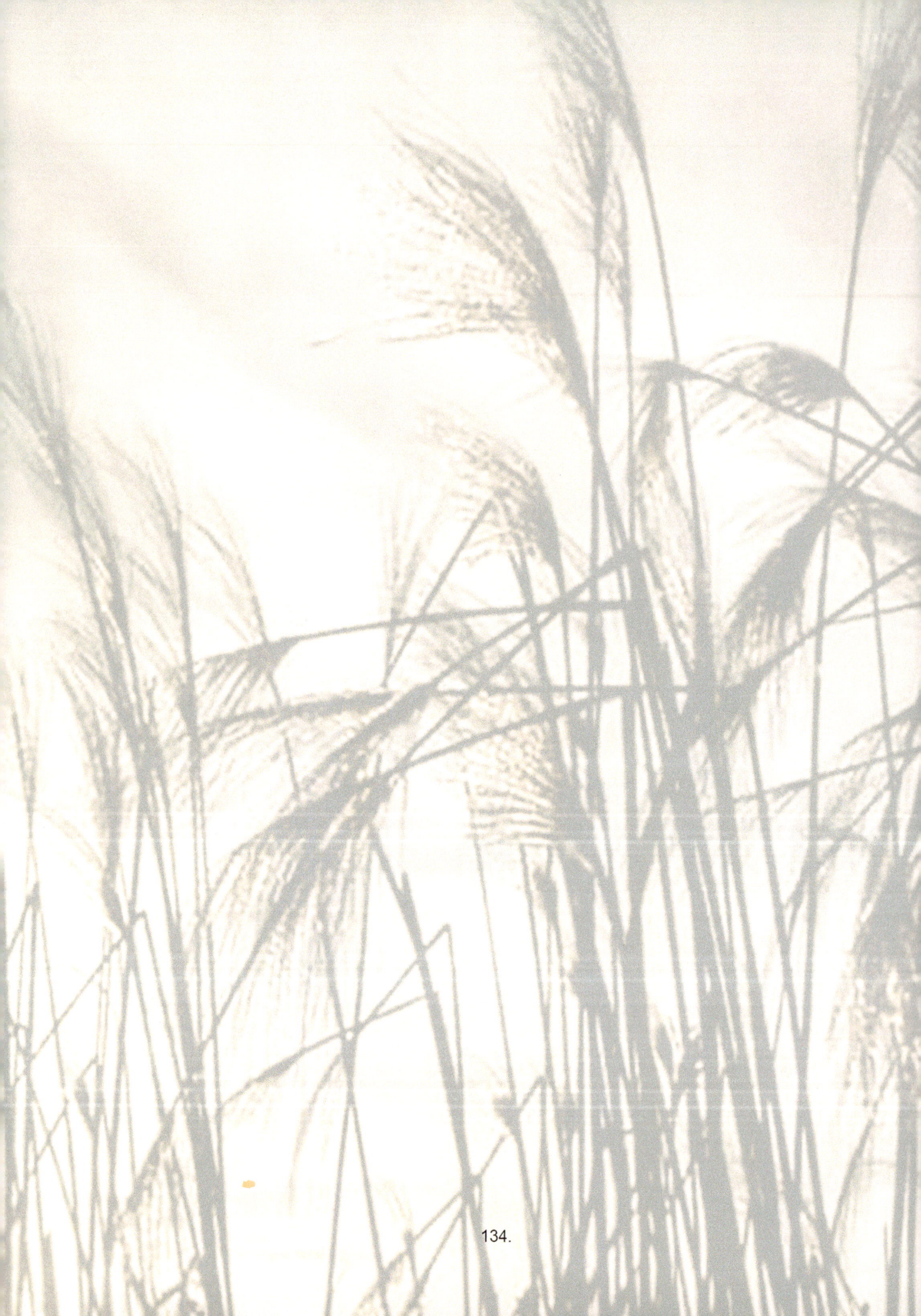

High Plains

You've been moving inward and listening. Now it's time to break free and unleash the truths of who you are.

Let me introduce you to the simplicity and rawness of the wide-open plains where it's ok to release.

In this pure, uninterrupted vastness, thoughts can flow freely. The air is different; it's fresh and unaffected, with only an occasional hawk's cry to break through the thin quiet breeze.

We can't always have these wide open plains to roam, but they can become symbols for your own wildness and clarity. There's a freedom to simplicity; it creates space to expand. There in the uncomplicated, you can unleash and reveal your true self to the world.

The art of being alive is simplifying, breaking free, and being who you are.

"Truth is found in simplicity, not in the multiplicity and confusion of things."
~Isaac Newton

Have you ever had the experience of watching wild horses run across the plains? It's breathtaking.

When I was shooting this particular wild herd in Wyoming, it created such a THRILL within me that it was hard to hold my camera still.

As I watched them in their natural environment, it reminded me that's what life is all about, an exhilarating gift of freedom every day.

We're free to get up, step out and chase our dreams.

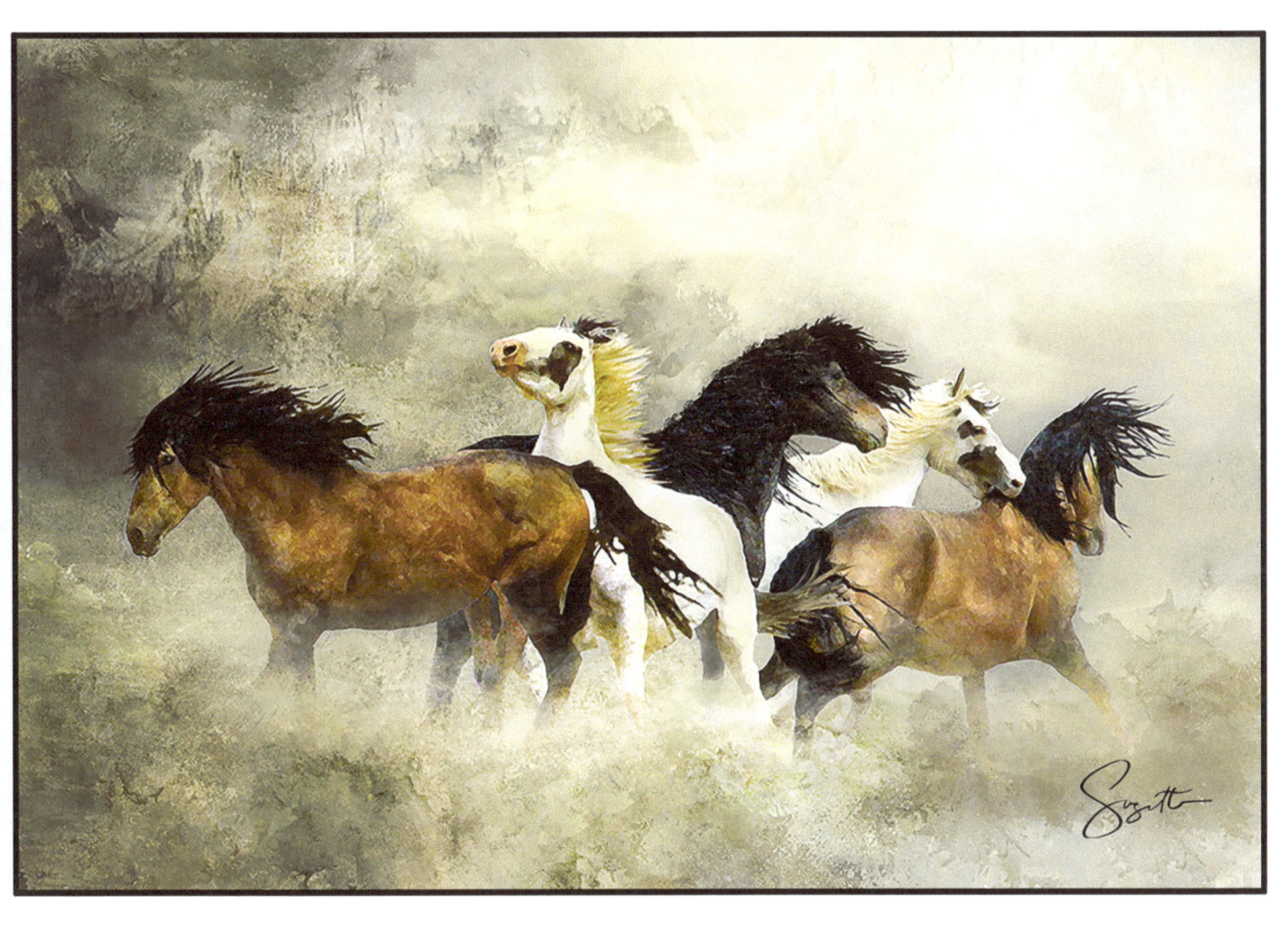

"Need nothing. Live passionately."
~unknown

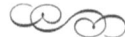

Vibrancy is waiting for you to step into every minute.

When you find your mind occupied
with unproductive earthly affairs,
allow your Inner Sanctuary
to scoop you into the realm of your Depths.

It's then and only then that you can begin to live.

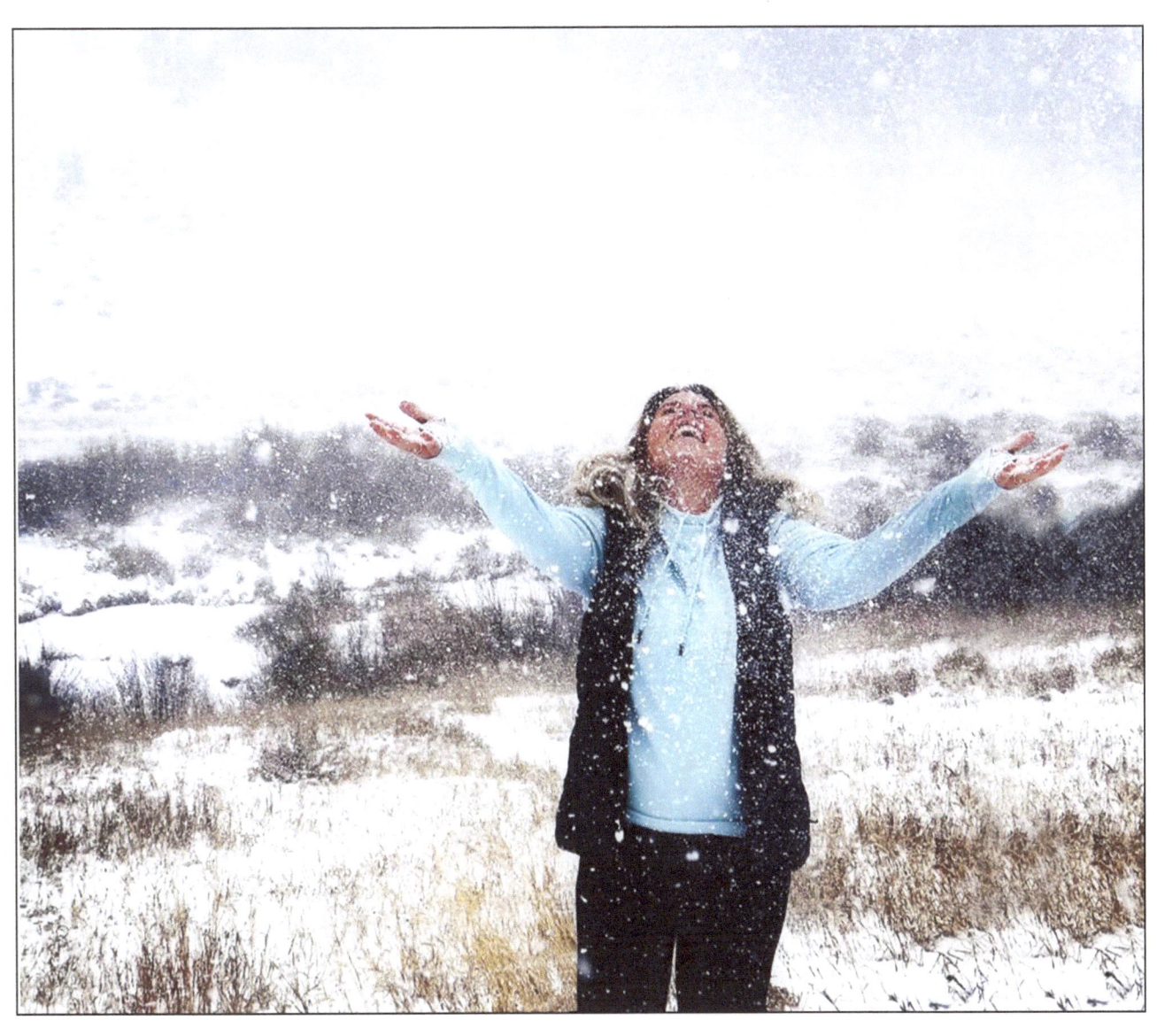

"Each moment that you're happy is a gift to the rest of the world."
~H.Palmer

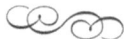

Stepping out and focusing on your Purpose is difficult when you're fearful and not sure of what each day holds.

Step forward anyway. Relax, let go and allow your Inner Voice to counsel you. When you do this, you'll feel an enormous sense of release and your Source will guide your every move.

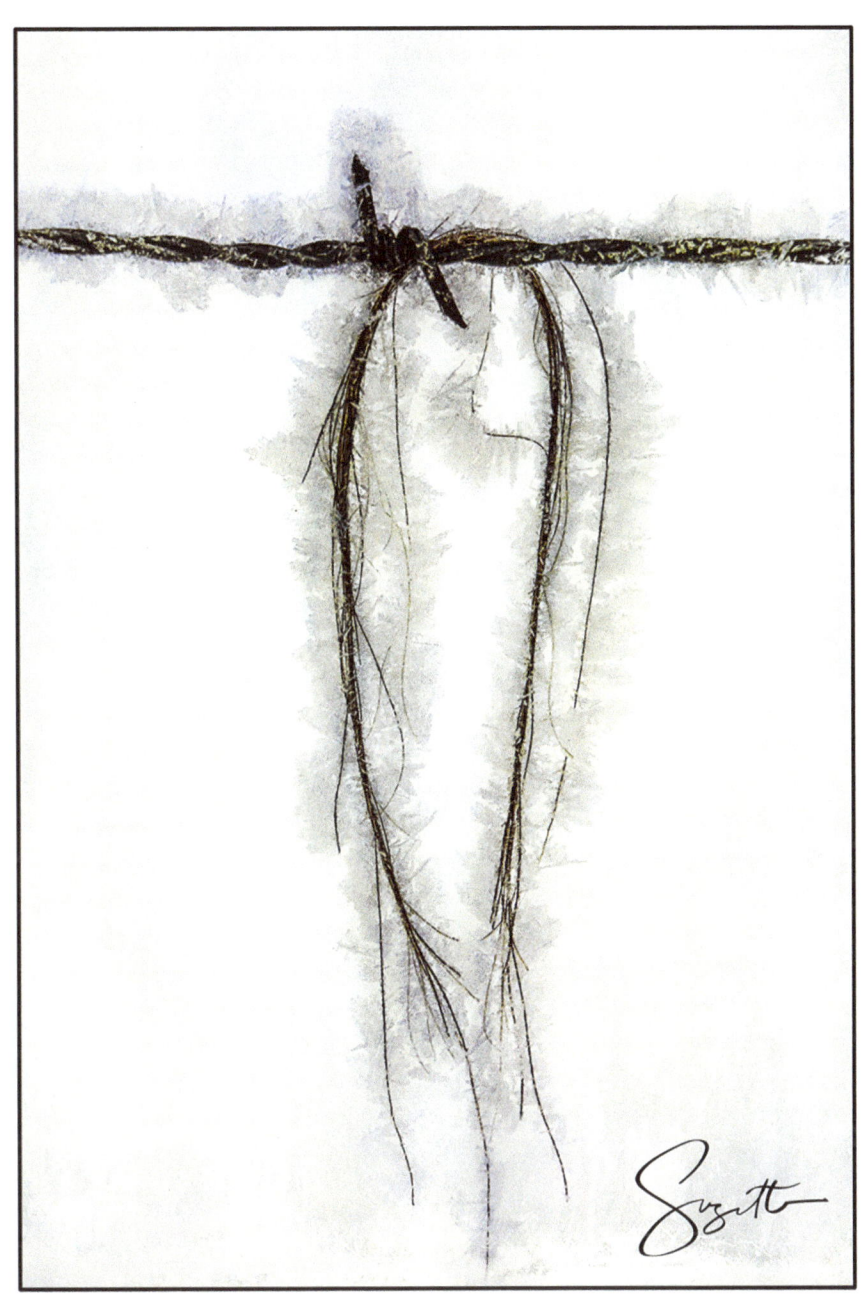

"Always do what you are afraid to do."
~Emerson

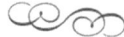

To capture the effect I wanted for this image, I waited in a dry riverbed below the dunes with a long lens and observed as the sun dropped into the Colorado evening sky. The shadows danced and moved with the sun, continually changing the dunes' contours and drama, moment by moment.

I shot hundreds of images that afternoon by staying put and allowing Mother Nature to reveal her splendor.

I wish I could relax and take the time to do this more often in my life. Sometimes I push too hard and forget how essential stillness is to creativity.

Moments like those in the riverbed remind me that life is simple. Why do we make it so complicated?

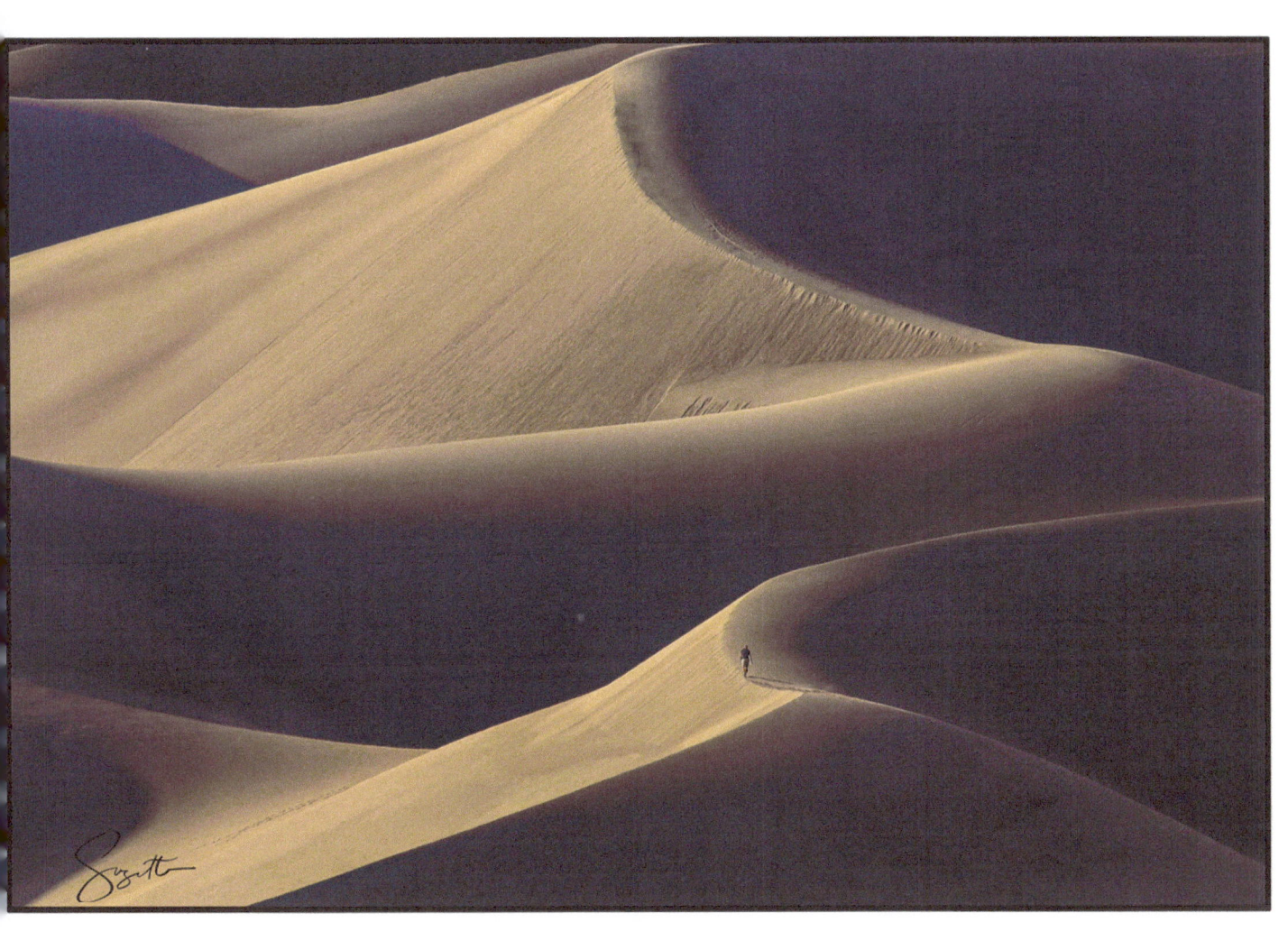

"Life is really simple but we insist on making it complicated."
~Confucius

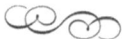

You can have it all -
energy, ecstasy, enterprise, *and* solitude.

It takes balance.
Never consuming yourself too much
but staying attuned to the world around you,
with a relentless focus on why you're here.

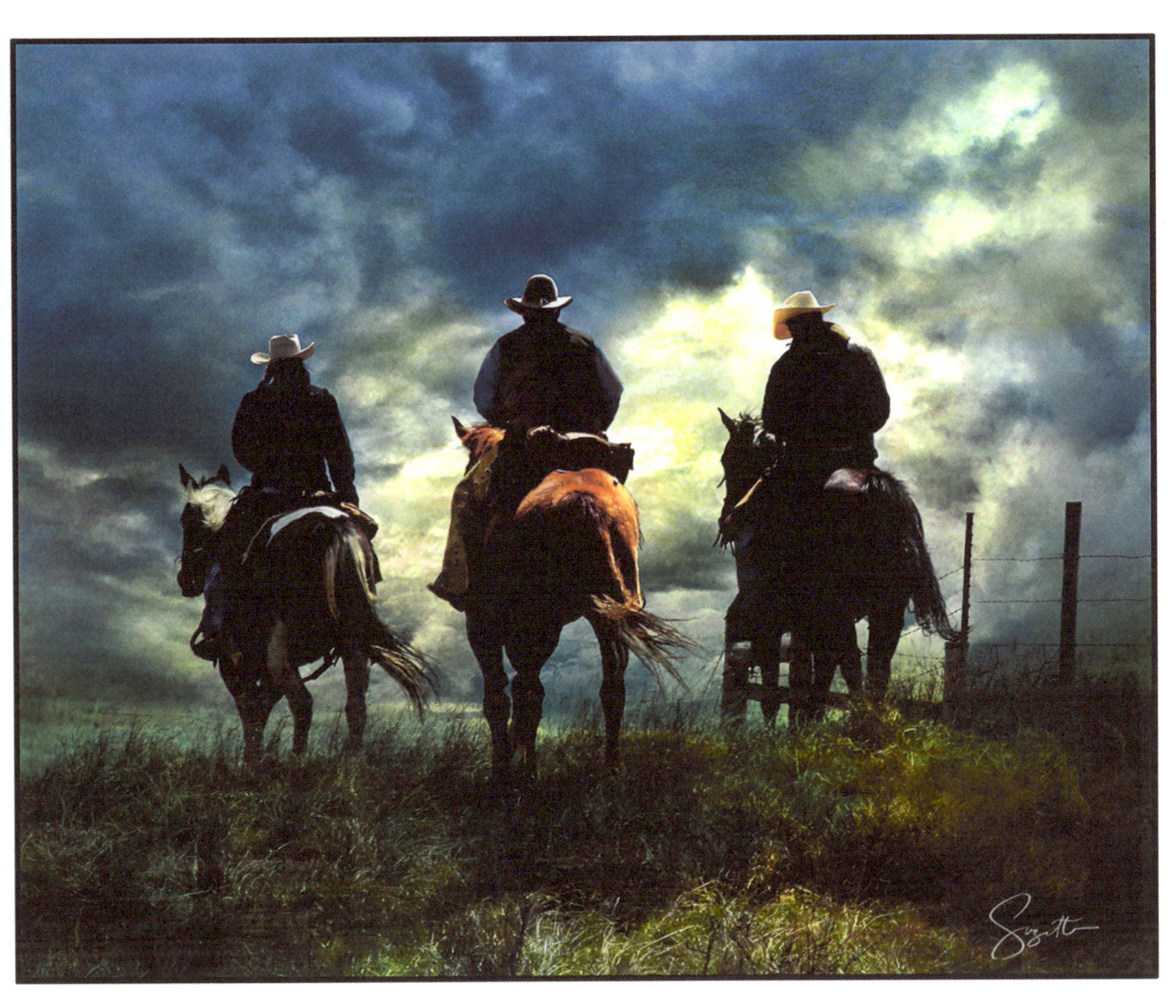

"*May you live all the days of your life.*"
~ Jonathan Swift

Feeling empty, lifeless, and disenchanted with where you are in life
is because you ignore your inner existence.

Move inward to YOU.

Expand into the strength of Spirit deep inside
and feel the exhilaration of this Presence within you.

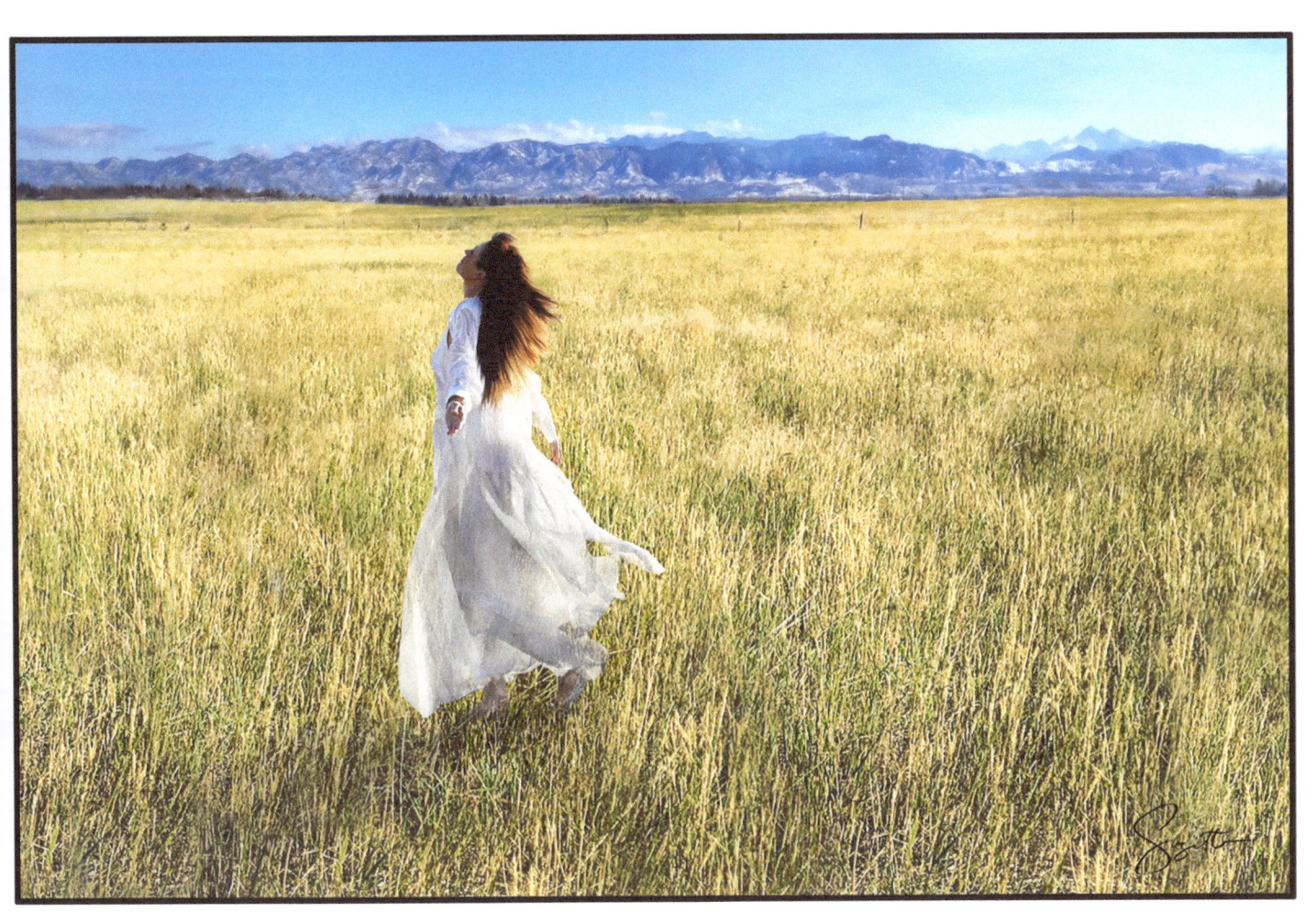

"Every day brings a chance for you to draw in a breath, kick off your shoes, and dance."
~ Oprah Winfrey

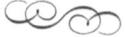

Just this morning, I tried this - hurling myself into the abyss.
I made the phone call I had feared to make, and guess what?
Great results happened.
Every time I propel myself forward instead of withdrawing,
I find magic on the other side.

What are we afraid of?

Hurl yourself forward.
Extraordinary things are about to happen.

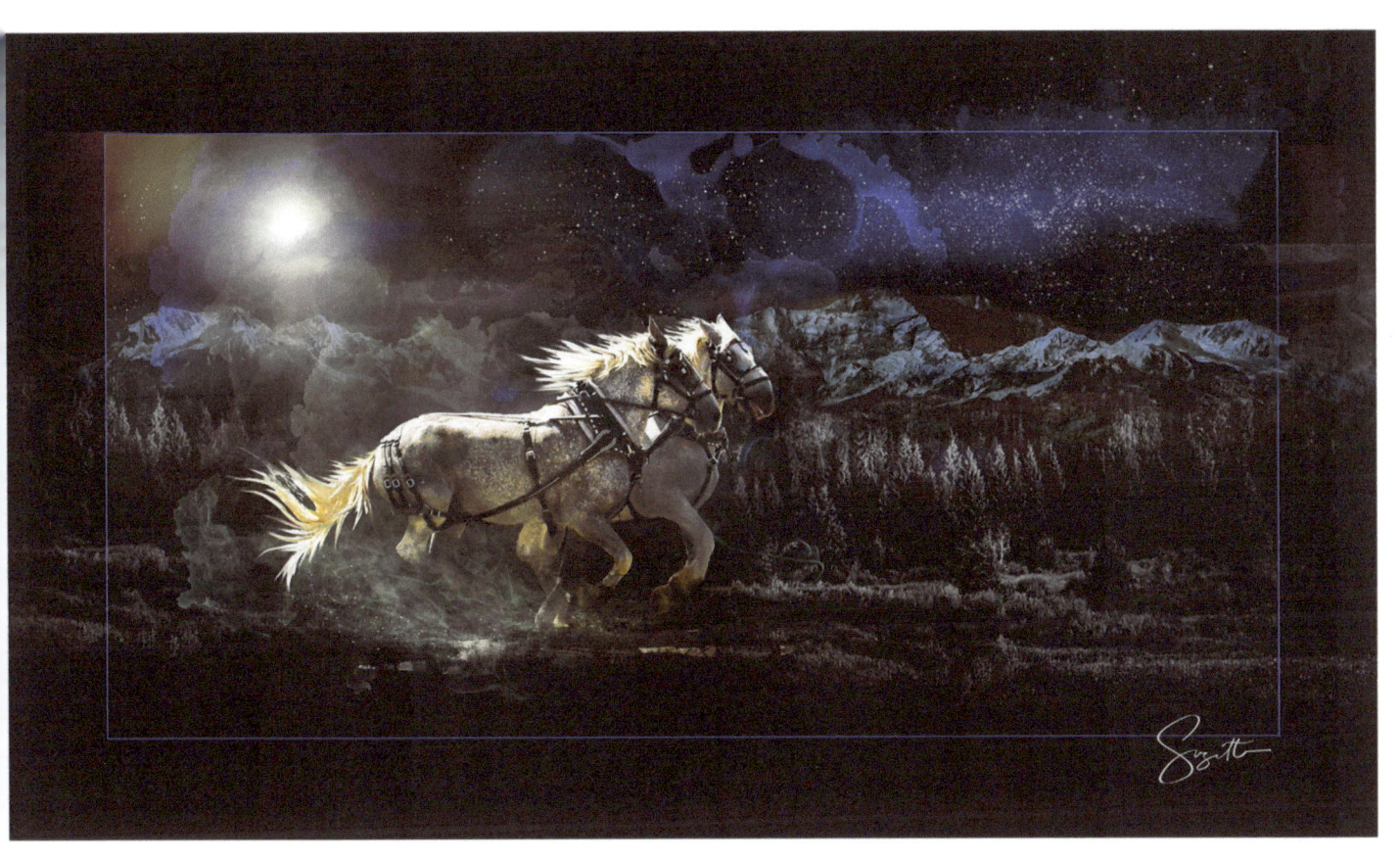

'Magic is done by throwing yourself into the abyss and discovering it's a featherbed."
~Terence Mckenna

Escape into the Vision of Inner Wisdom, and you'll move from what you've always known into unexplored territory. Growth takes place every time you look inward, open up and trust your instincts.

Retreat to the power of your Source and then release back out into the world.

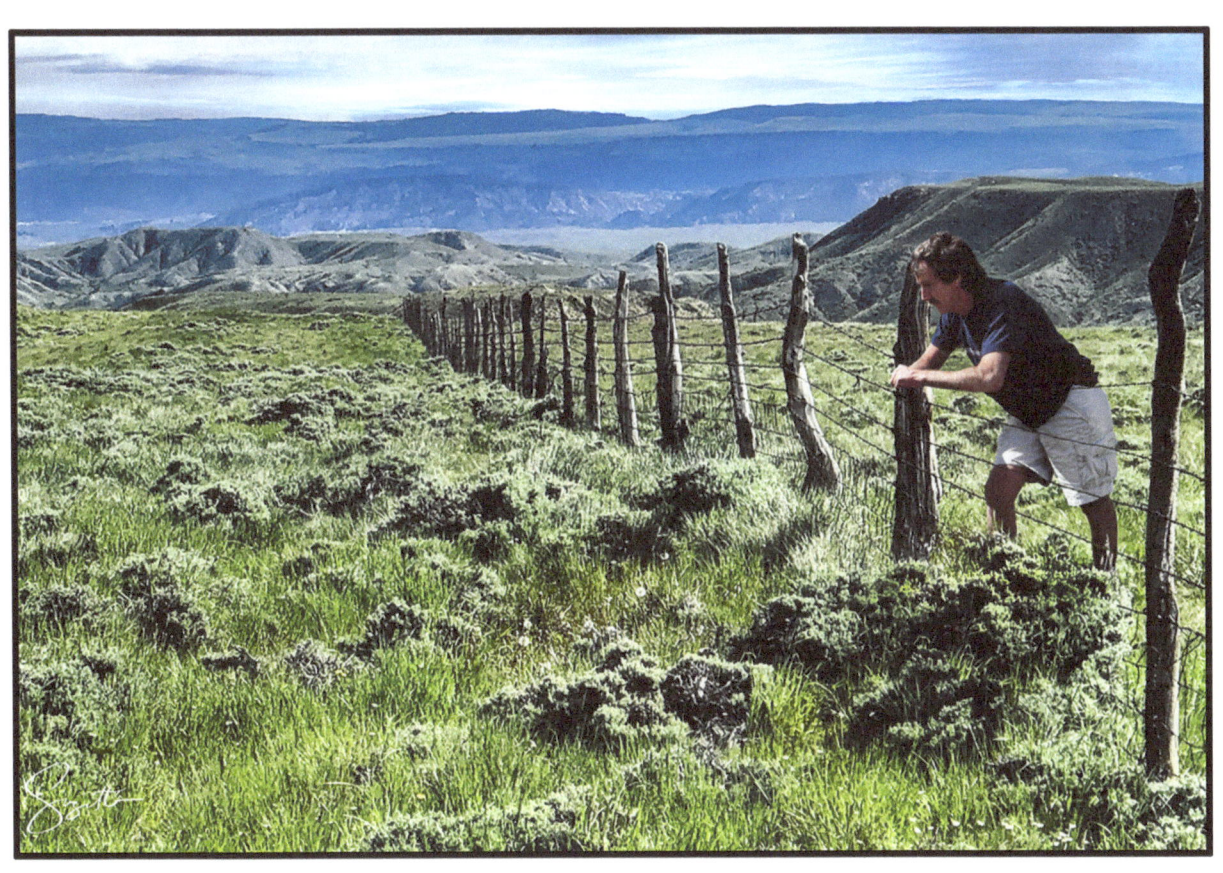

"Man can learn nothing except by going from the known to the unknown."
~ Claude Bernard

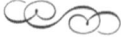

This thought is about needing less is freeing.
It releases expectations
so we can roam through the day giving,
instead of waiting to receive.

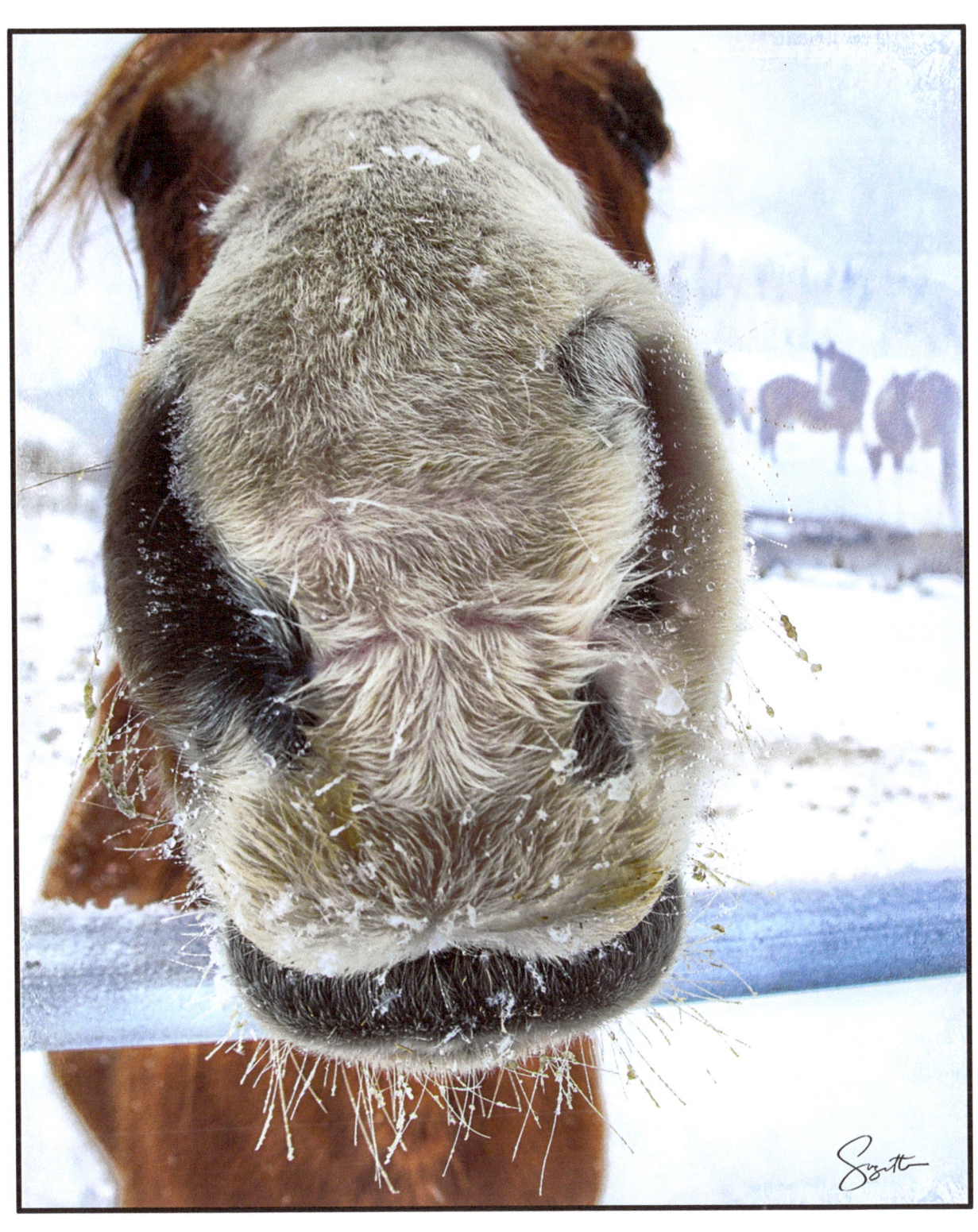

"All you need is less."
~unknown

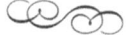

Enjoying more by needing less.
The place of perfect peace.

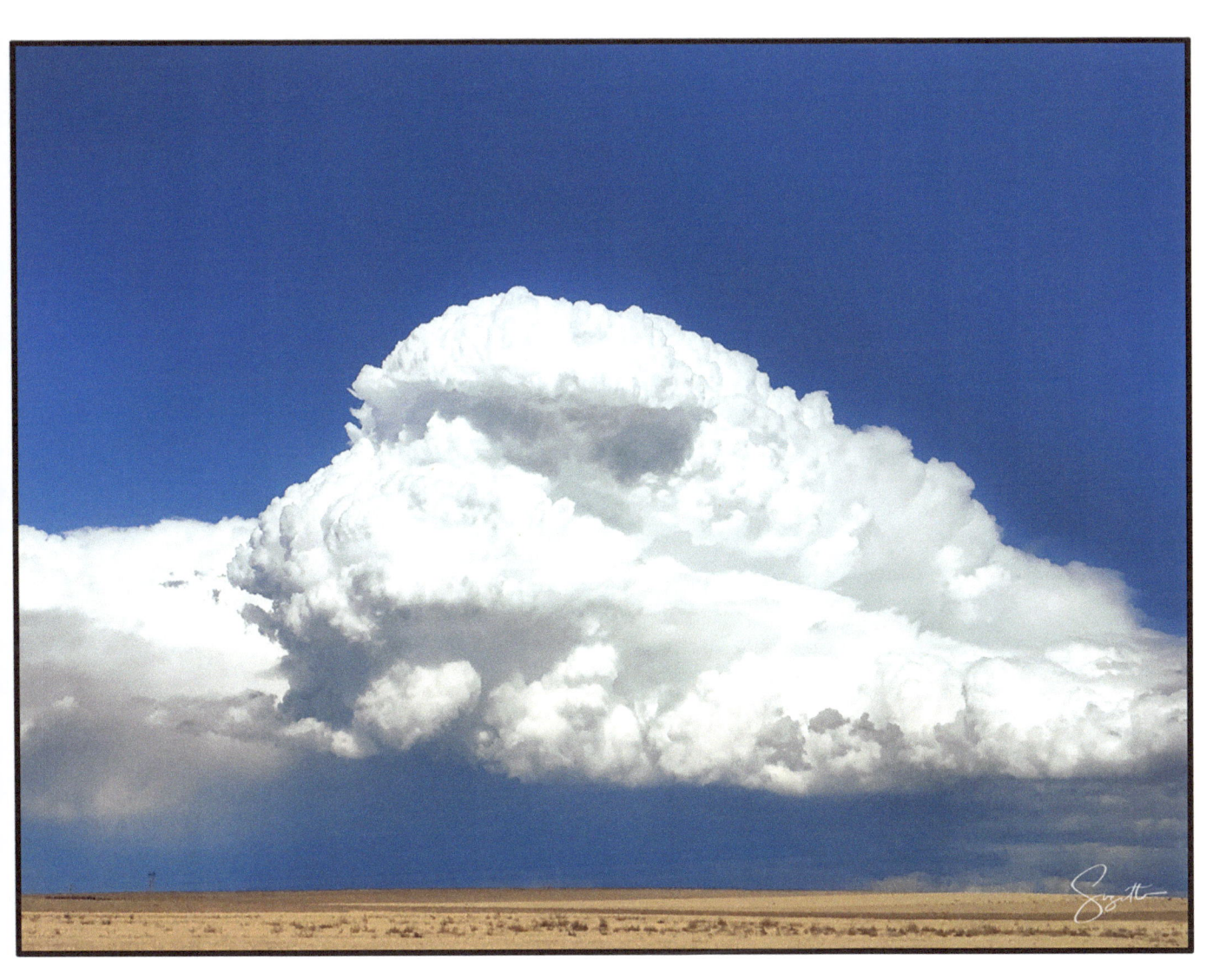

"Very little is needed to make a happy life."
~Marcus Aurelius

Sometimes illness must come to slow us down and learn to appreciate wellness. In healing, we experience a heightened awareness level, as if coming out of the clouds and into the sunshine.

With a cleared head, there's new energy and crisp vision, moving in and out of other's lives as a fresh breeze, quietly and without hesitation, adding vibrancy to everything in our path.

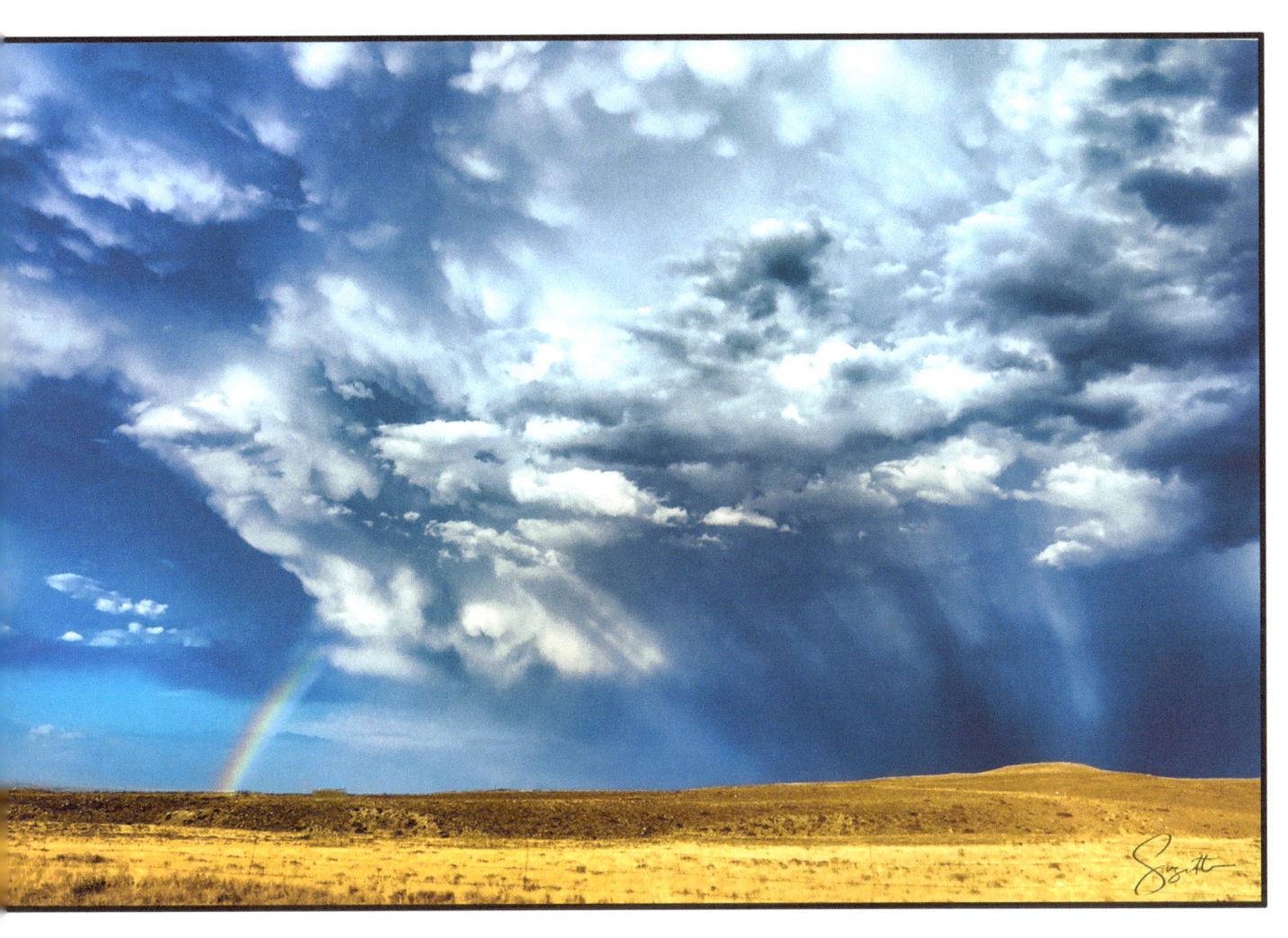

"Clouds come floating into my life, no longer to carry rain,
but to add color to my sunset sky."
~Rabindranath Tagore

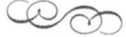

Fear comes within the boundaries of limitation.
There are no limits to the Universe within you.
Feel this strength expanding you with vibrant energy
and venture out into the world.
There is no separation.
There are no limits.

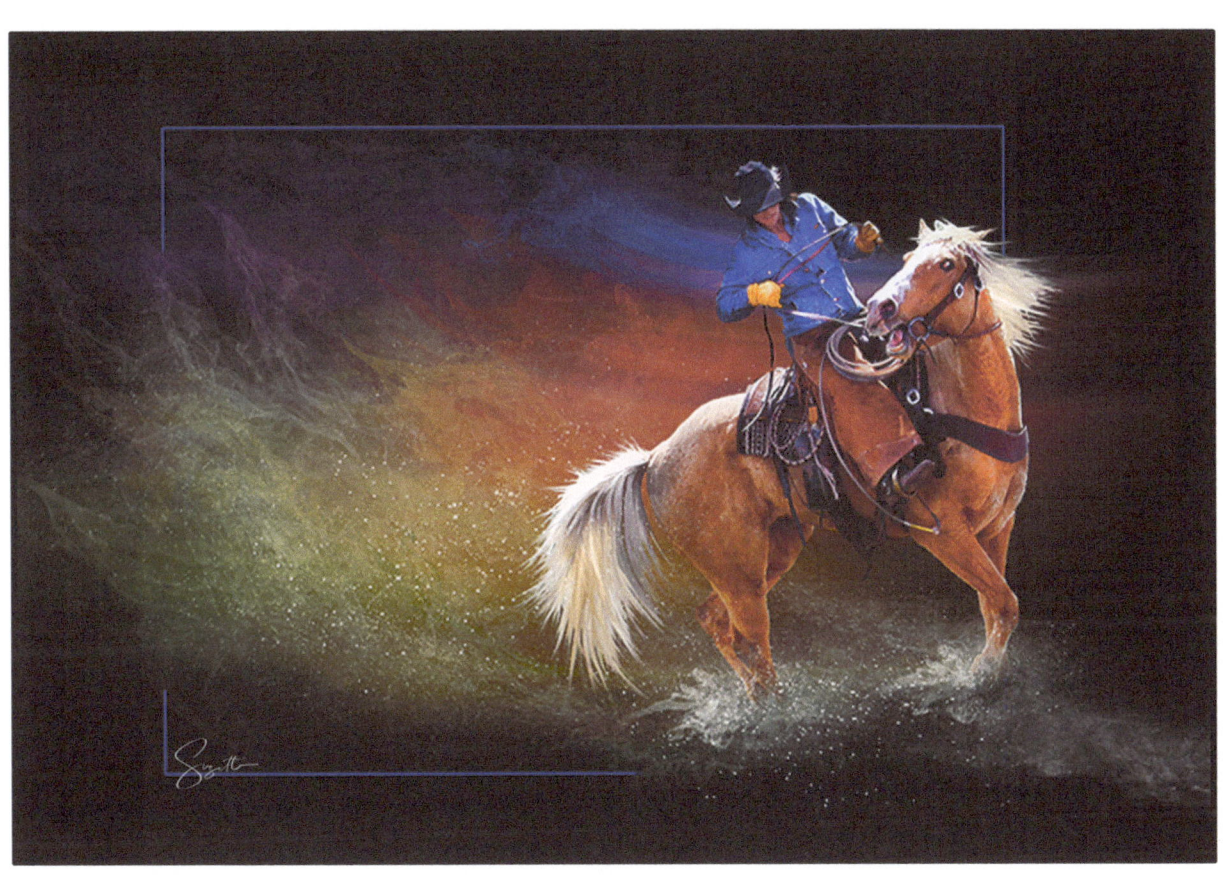

"No difficulty can dishearten the man who has acquired the art of being alive."
~Ella Wheeler Wilcox

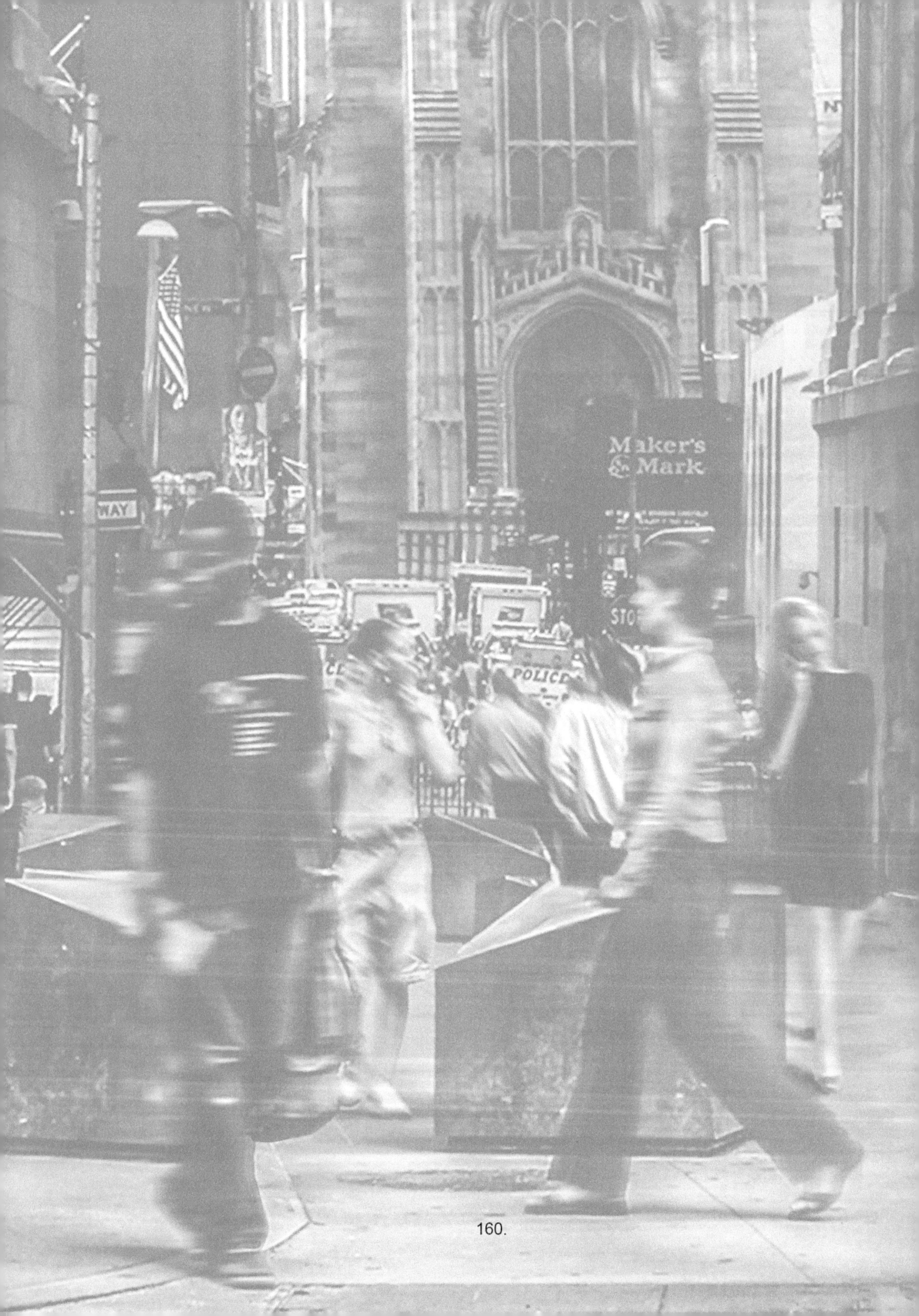

PEOPLE

You don't exist alone. There comes a time when you need to take the knowledge gained from your inward journey and expand it out into life.

It's too easy to tuck this Inner Spirit away and fall back into the old way, moving through the clamor of the day on autopilot. But think of what the world can gain from you when you turn inward to God, your Wellspring, and then step outward into each day.

This chapter is about working from your Source.

The art of being alive is weaving your Deepest Self back out into the world.

"To affect the quality of the day, that is the highest of arts."
~Henry David Thoreau

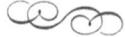

There will be those who need your peaceful presence
and your unfaltering strength.

As you have become a part of Nature in your times of solitude,
try becoming part of those who need you,
working deep into their inner souls to comfort them.

Comfort them as Nature comforts you,
all the while remaining elevated from your Inner Light.

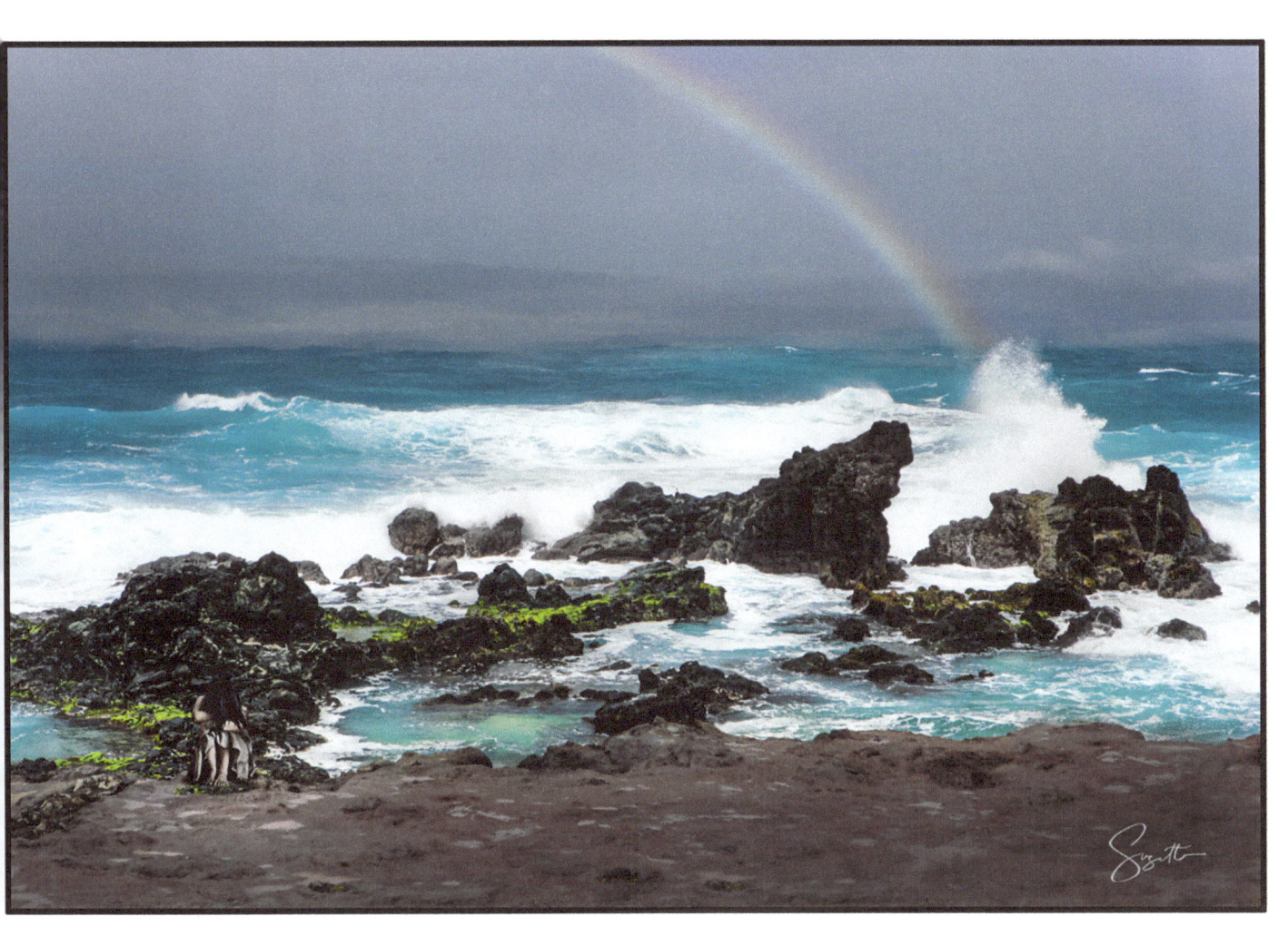

"*Try to be a rainbow in someone's cloud*".
~*Maya Angelou*

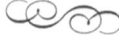

What you do for a living is only part of your work on earth.
Never let it consume you to the point of missing your purpose.
Expand into each moment,
radiating goodness to all who are in your presence.

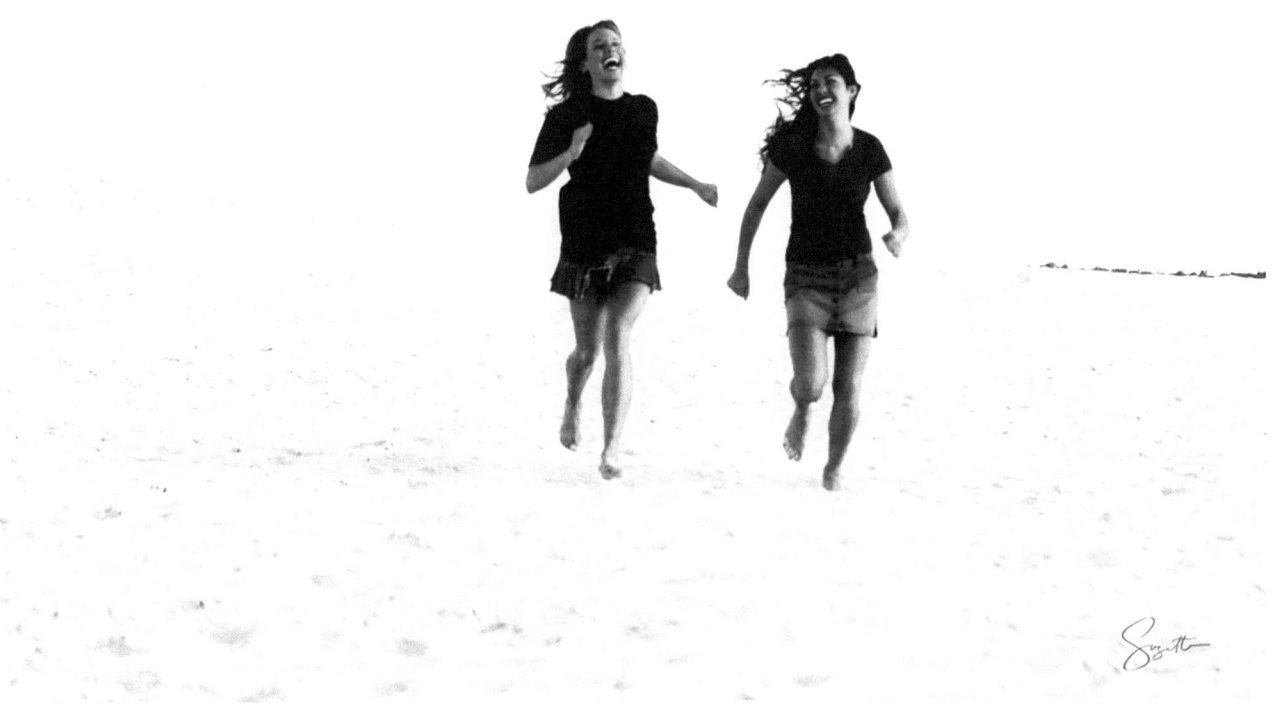

*"There are two great days in a person's life -
the day we are born and the day we discover why."
~William Barclay*

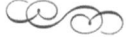

There's no need to look for things that are larger than life.

There's extraordinary in the ordinary,
but you must quiet yourself enough to find it.

Seeing life through your Internal eyes,
the world becomes astonishing, magnificent, and beautiful.

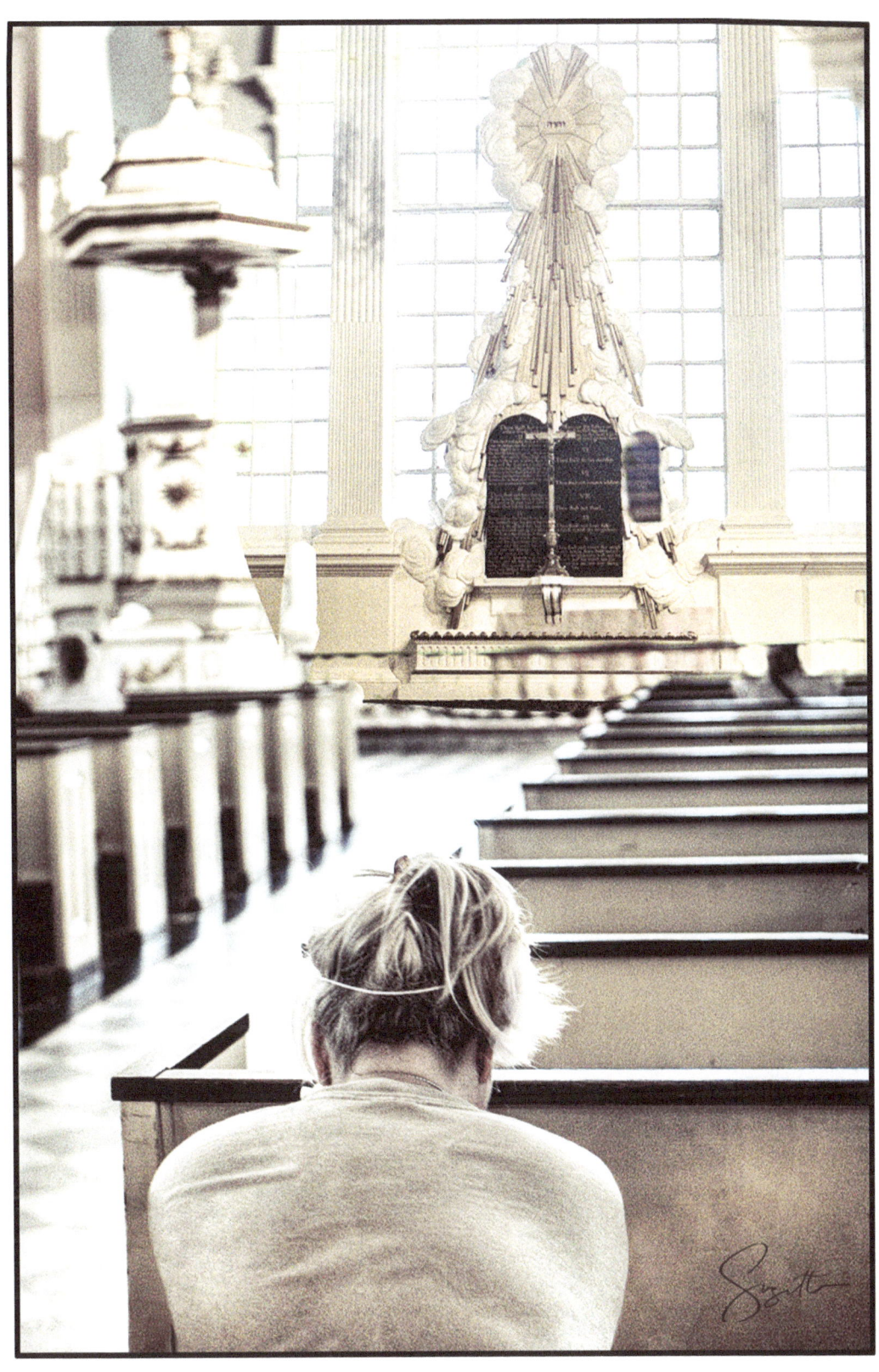

"Let my life be a work of art."
~Eric Overby

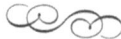

When you're in tune with your surroundings, it changes your expression.
When you're present, your Infinite Self moves through your smile
the same way rays move through the sun,
casting light into the darkness of another's soul.

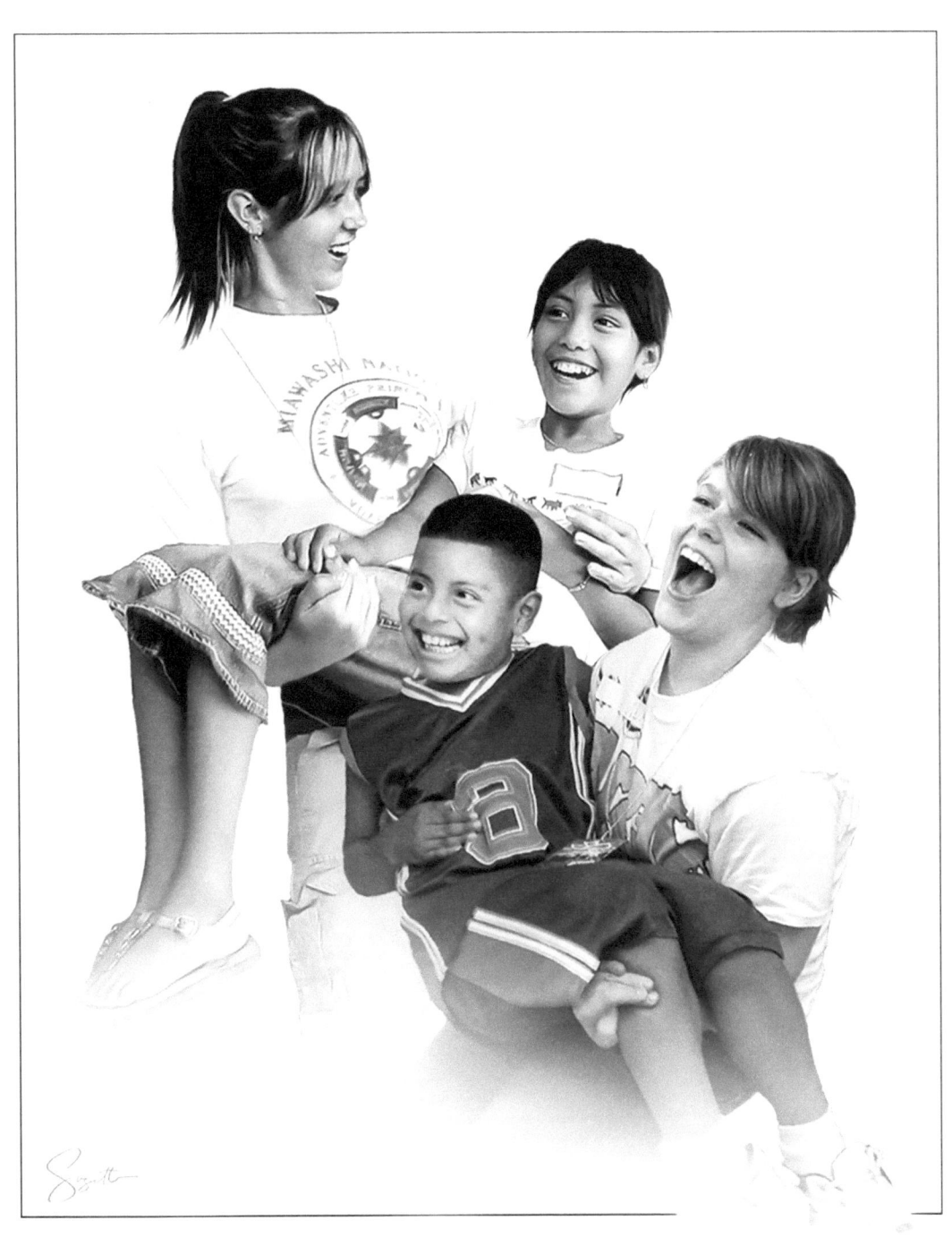

"The greatest gift you can give someone is your presence."
~ Thich Nhat Hanh

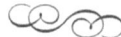

There are times when you have just enough drive to make it through the day. Reaching out and spending energy on things other than what you already have planned sounds like more than you can handle.

With a consistent Channel from the Greater Power within, you will feel an endless source of Energy flowing through you. God gives to you so you can give to others.

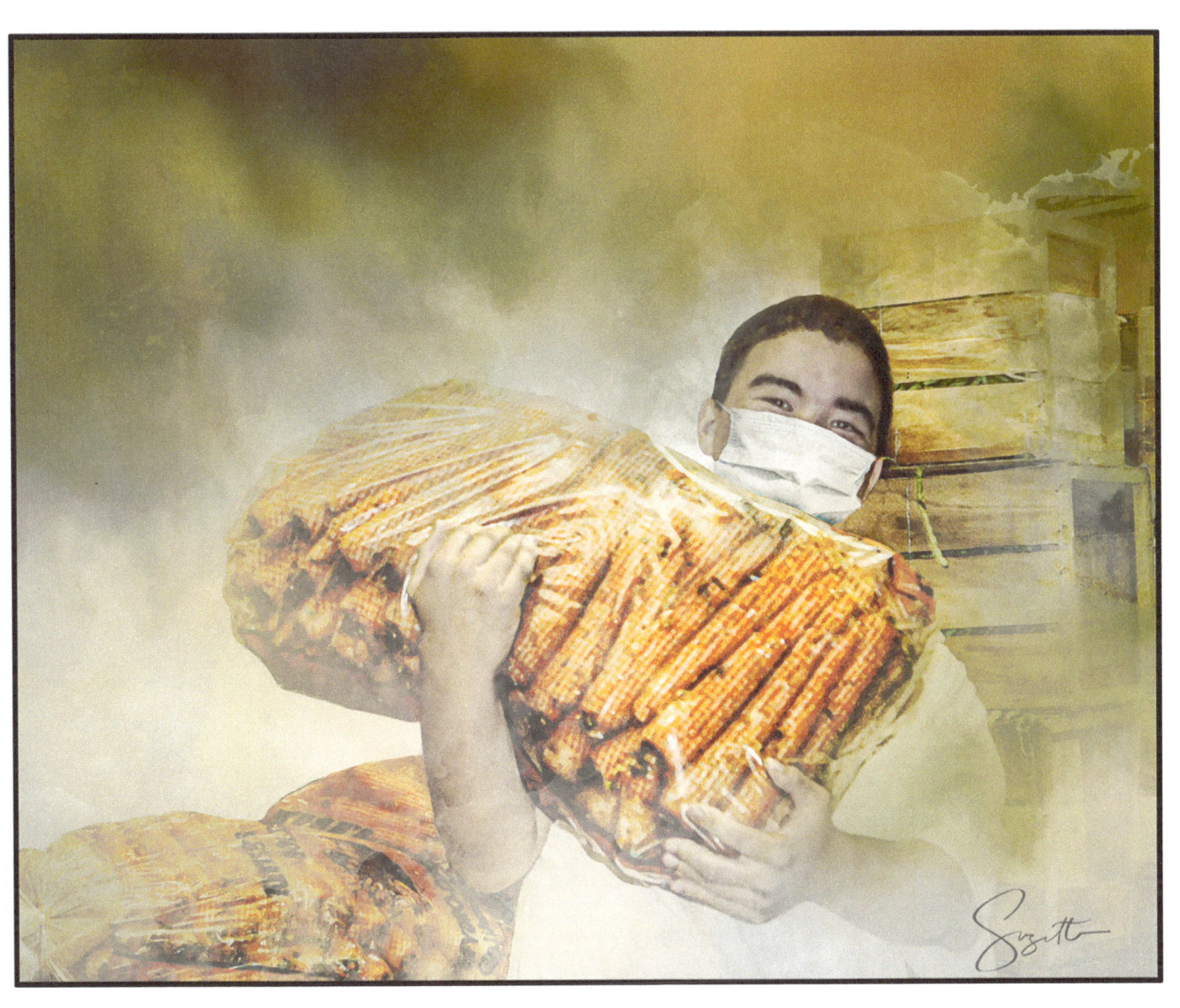

"God has given us two hands, one to receive with and the other to give with."
~Billy Graham

Sometimes just being available is all that's needed;
present enough for someone to feel
the significance of their worth.

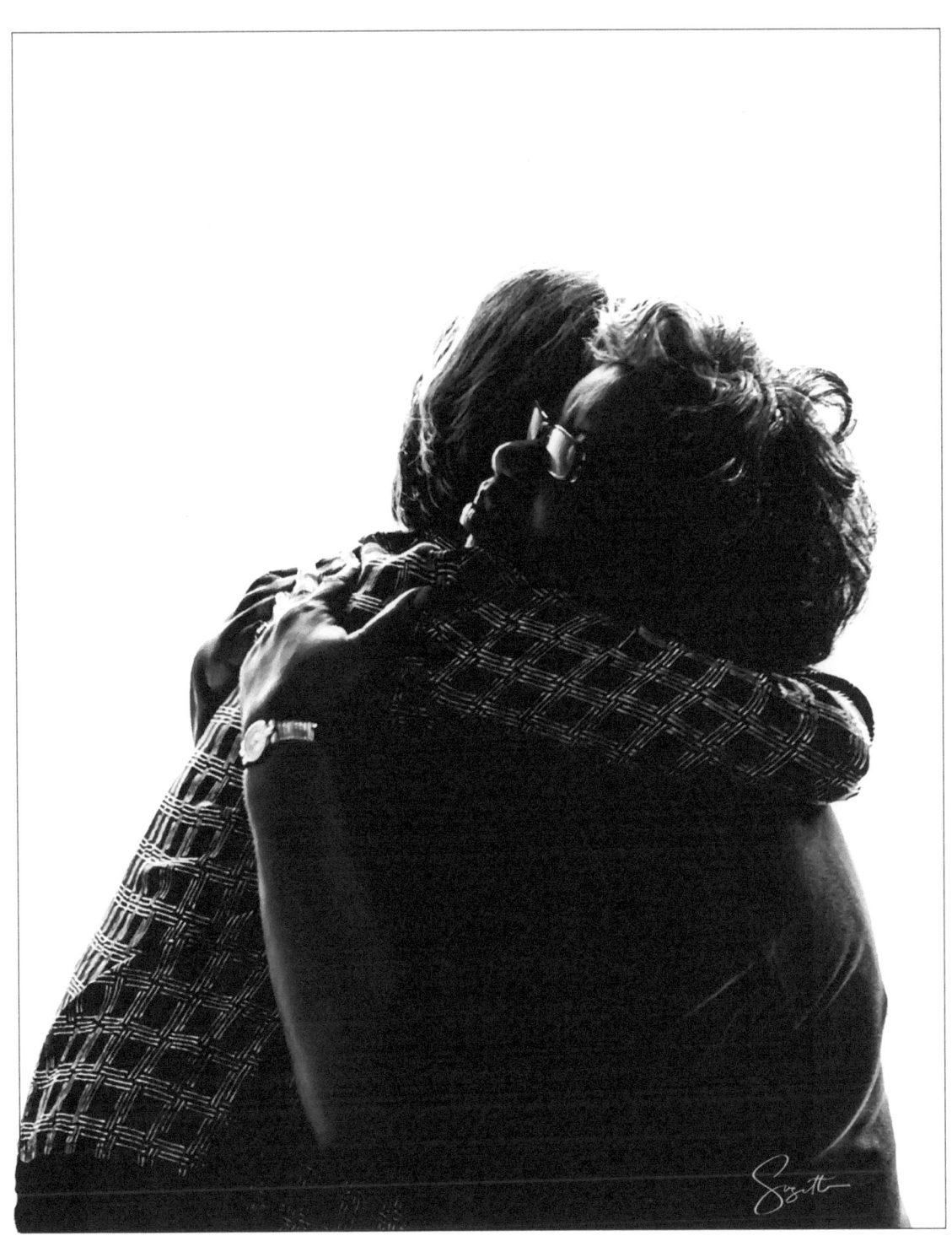

"Leave everyone better than you found them."
~ Robin Sharma

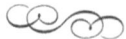

You'll make a difference in someone's life
if your encounter is about them, not you.

Surrendering the attention isn't easy.
It's a natural tendency to want others to know about you,
but it's usually at the expense of their needs.

Disintegrate yourself.
Reach inward to move outward.
Your Inner Sanctuary will take care of your needs,
so you can be present enough for theirs.

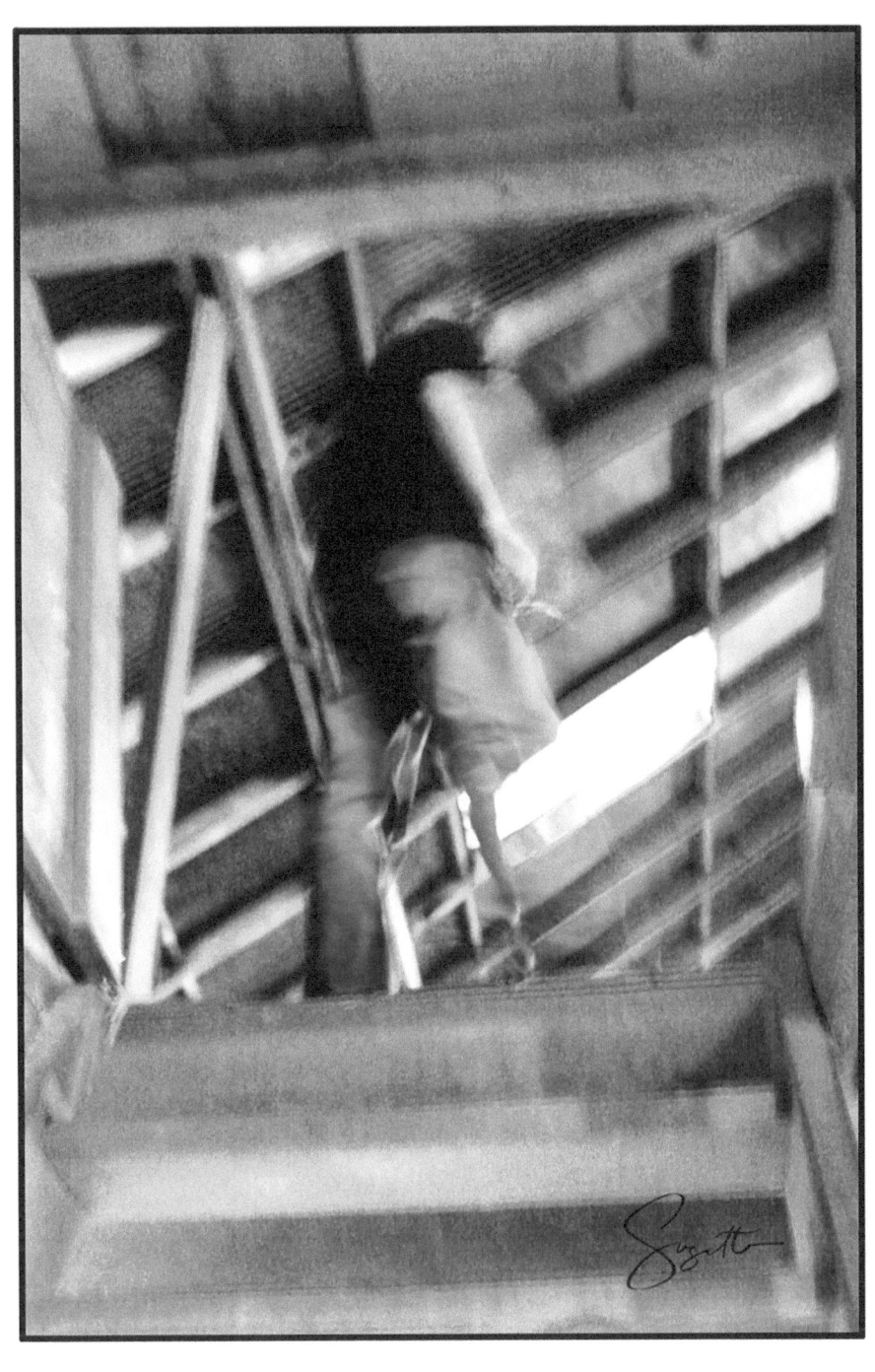

"Never strive to make your presence noticed, just make your absence felt."
~ Grace Lichtenstein

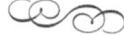

There is a common thread that connects everyone on earth - the need to feel complete.

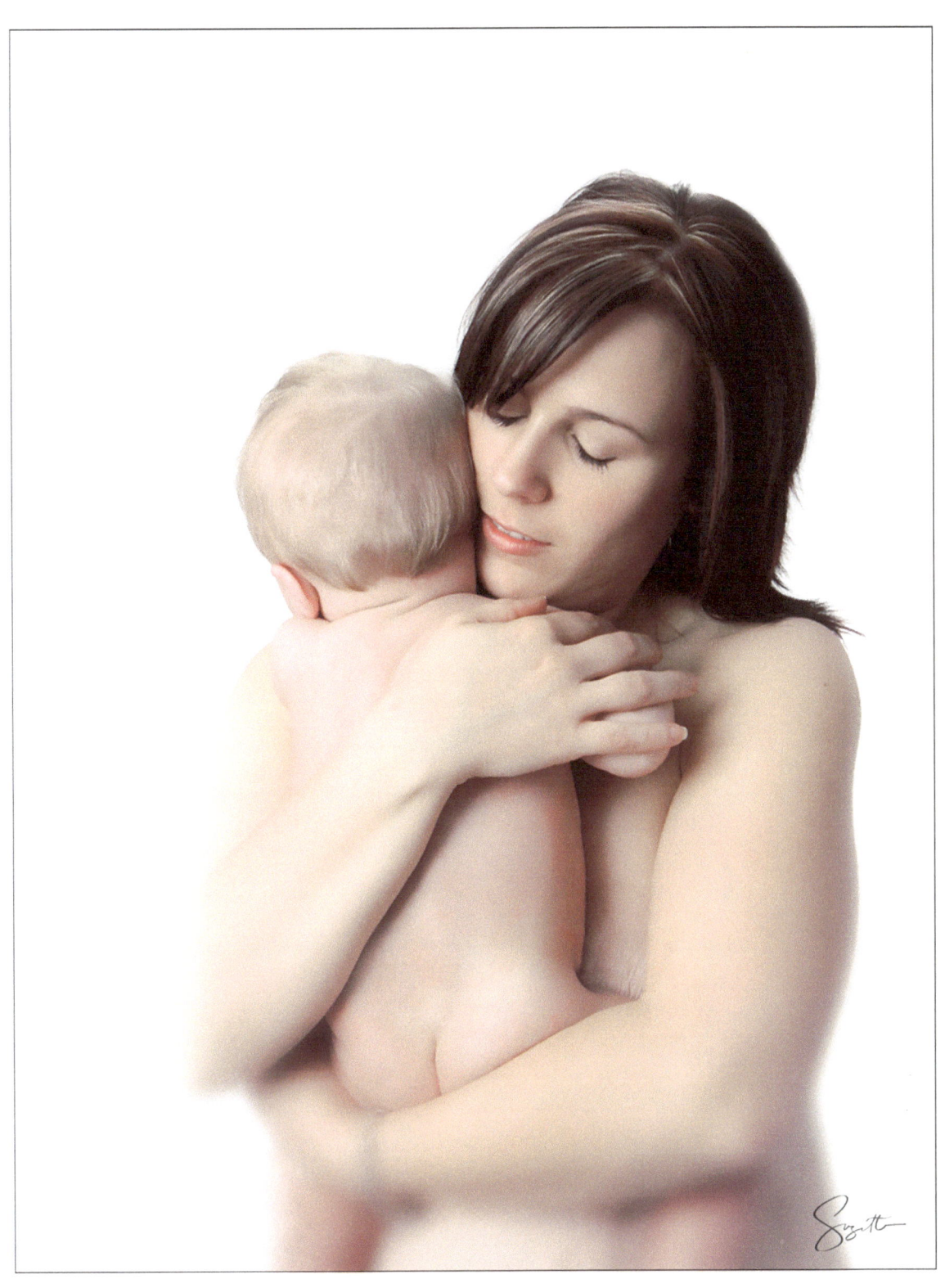

"Man is harder than rock and more fragile than an egg."
~Yugoslav Proverb

Do you find that being around people who are contiually resentful and discontent to be draining?

Remember this: negativity is based on fear.

A cynical person has nothing to fear with you because your Source from within is pure love, pure strength, pure protection.

Shift inward to work outward.
Love dissipates fear.

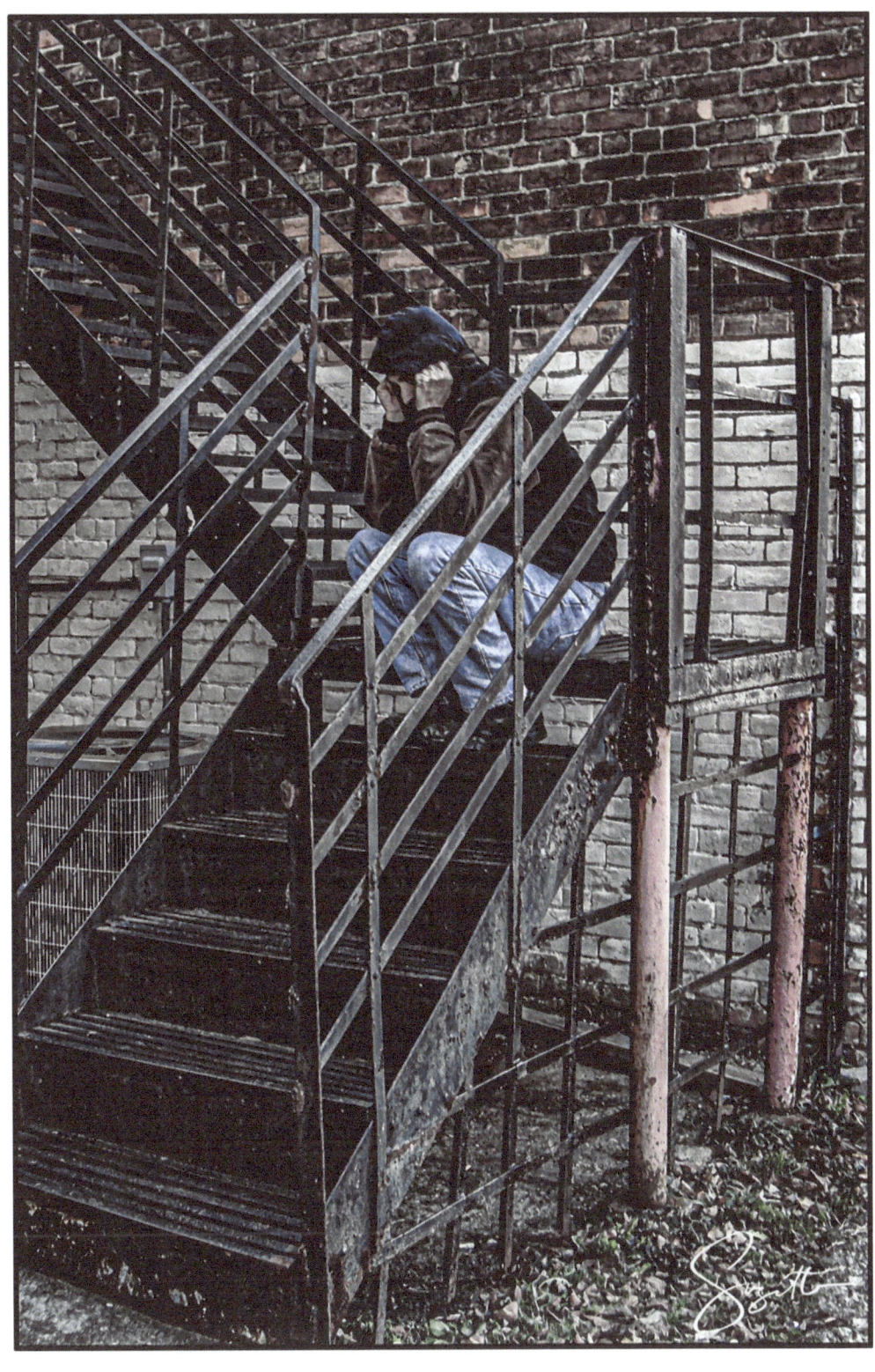

"Our job is to love others without stopping to inquire whether or not they are worthy."
~Thomas Merton

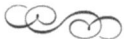

Your mind has complete control of whether you're
reponsive or closed to the world.
Allow yourself to open up.
Let go. Let yourself flow into life around you.
Share your passion. Share your love. Share your empathy.

Add something to everything you touch.

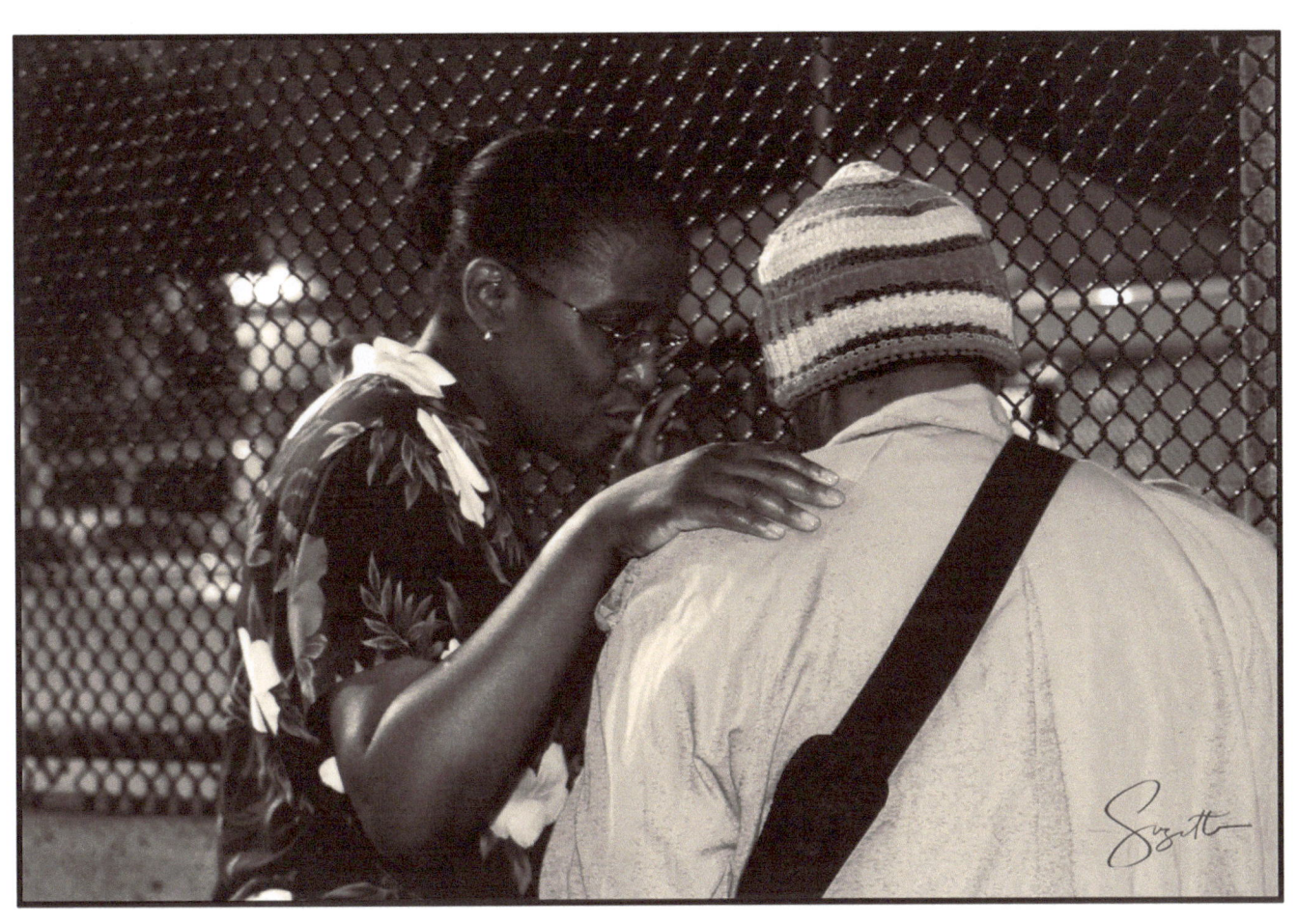

"Vow to live fully in each moment and to look at all beings with eyes of compassion."
~ Thich Nhat Hanh

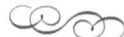

We wear ourselves thin trying to keep up with the life we've created. A life of contentment can't happen with consumption and speed. They contradict. Consumption is the opposite of satisfaction. The more you have, the more you desire.

Desire interferes with fulfillment. Desire interferes with happiness. Desire interferes with reaching out to others.

Time has disappeared.

The pandemic forced us into our homes, and this isolation gave us back the gift of time. We had space to reflect. We began to look inward, upward, and then sideways to each other.

We began reaching out to help instead of reaching out for more.

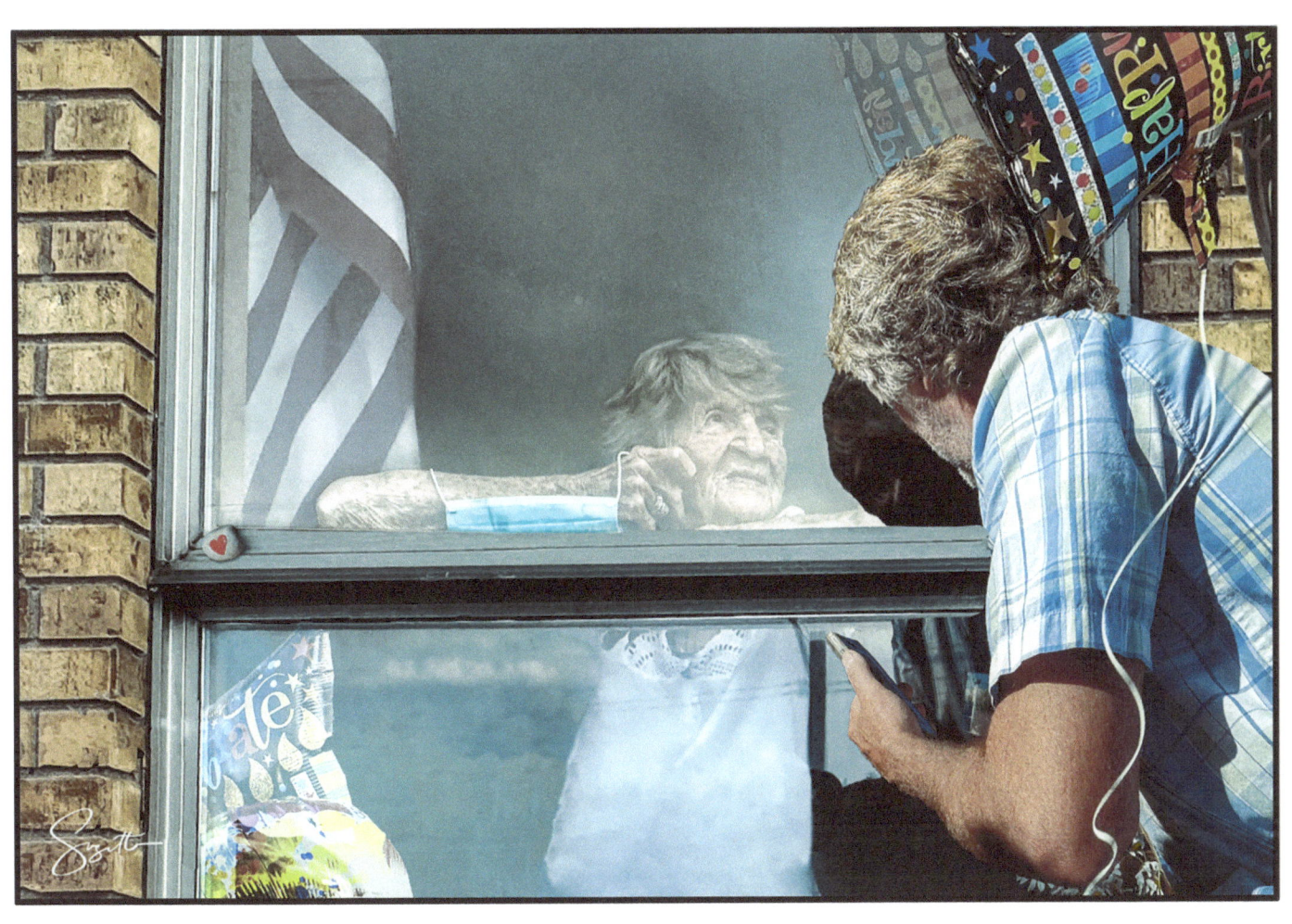

"We change the world not by what we do,
but as a consequence of what we have become."
~ David Hawkins

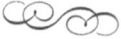

Go out into the world and shine.
Remember I Am with you
and will watch over you wherever you go.
I will not leave you until I have done what I have promised you.

Genesis 28:15

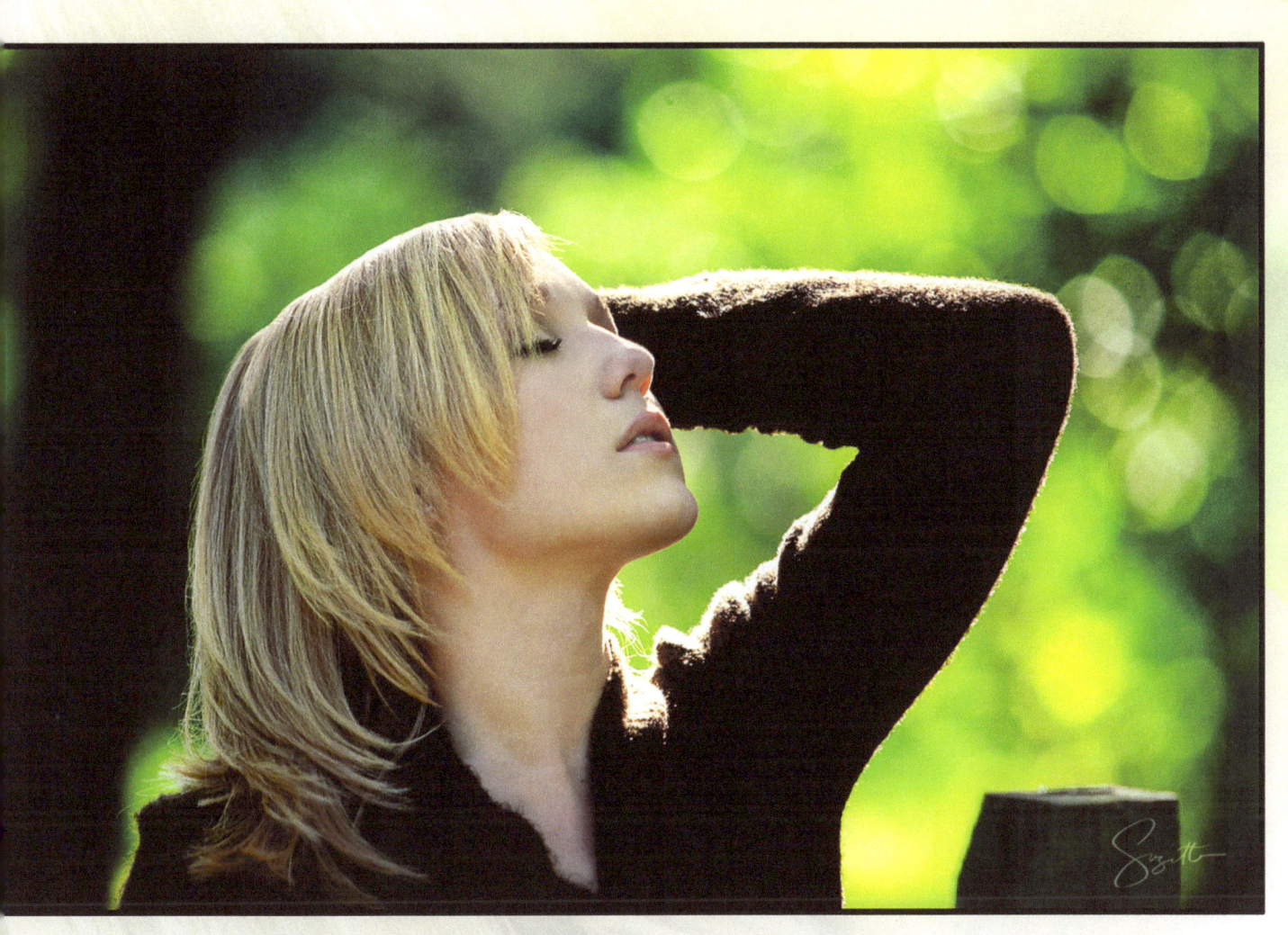

"Within you is the light of a thousand suns."
~ Robert Adams

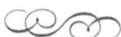

Suzette McIntyre is an award-winning artist and has been recognized internationally for her signature style of photography.

She began her profession as a photographer in the early 90's when studying creative writing in college and began working in genres, from weddings and portraiture to landscape and eventually fine art.

Suzette views photography as a relationship and an art. Through her studies, she discovered that combining her writing with her connection to the image added a new dimension to the overall impact of the finished piece. Blending the three creates her distinctive, intimate style.

Her canvases and photography, inspired by her deep passion for people and love of the western wilderness, can be seen in galleries throughout Colorado and Wyoming.

Suzette has also co-authored a series of words & images coffee table books, including 'Beauty Surrounds Us', 'The Paths We Take', and 'Reflection', all available on Amazon.

More information and works can be found at: https://www.PhotographyBySuzette.com and her blog, "The Art of Living" at: https://www.PhotographyBySuzette.org

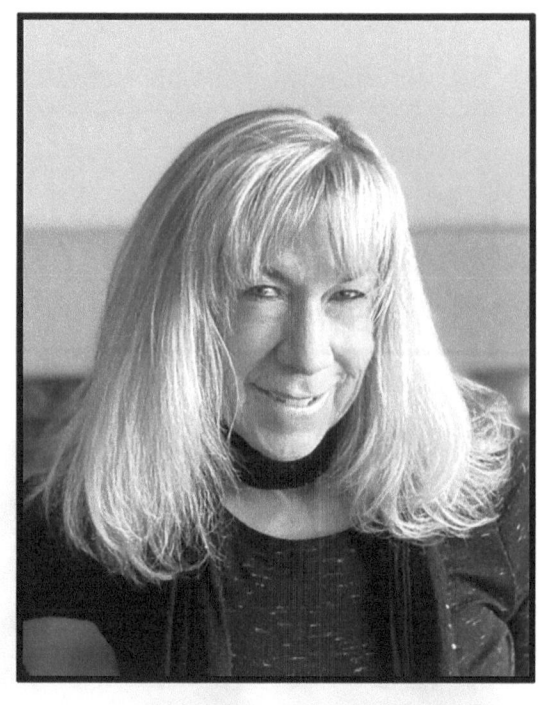

*Suzette McIntyre
Author, The Art of Being Alive*

Author's note about this book: I'm a Christian and believe the Spiritual Presence within me is Christ, the Holy Spirit, who connects us to God, the Ultimate Universal Power. I believe that it's His word within me, guiding and nourishing me daily. Yet, I also understand there are many other systems of belief, and respect the theologies that fulfill the same intention: Humanity. Kindness to ourselves and to one another until we meet again in Paradise.

ACKNOWLEDGEMENTS

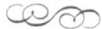

This book exists because of a few people in my life. They know who they are but I want you to know them too, because if you ever have the chance to encounter them yourself, their mere presence will enrich your life.

Jim McIntyre, my husband who breathed life into me as I breathed this book into existence.

Alex Demaree, my daughter, my friend who adds aliveness and vibrancy to every day of my life.

LeAnn Thieman, my driving force, and friend. Her cabin in Red Feather, Colorado, is where it all began.

Toby Baker, Susan Nelson, and Annie Surbeck: my stellas, my stars, whose creative energy feeds me daily.

Becky Schauss Bulfer, my lifetime friend, and judicial eye.

Pam Ingle and Janie Trimmer, my angels, and unending support.

Melinda Boddicker, whose yoga sessions and insights give me balance.

Woody Walters, whose mentorship continually encourages me to reach for new heights artistically.

Kerrie Flanagan, whose publishing expertise has been invaluable.

A special thanks to our models: Kristin Logue, Alexandra Demaree, Carole Sondrup, Ron English, Lauren Winnyk, Sahar Ullery, Jan Tiffany, Lindsey A. Cline, Kelsey Kline, Ryan Dobbins, Julia Milne, Muriel English, Emily Decker, and the other beautiful souls who inspired segments of this book.

> The Art of Being Alive is dedicated to my mother, Muriel English, who has given me a lifetime of confidence through her eternal belief in me, and who helped me trust the infinite Power of God.

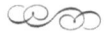

"Life has passed through me and become the gentle space in which my spirit dances."

~ Suzette

Printed in the USA
CPSIA information can be obtained
at www.ICGtesting.com
JSHW040206310723
44626JS00011BB/9